# Reach for the Racquet

*To Para-badminton*
*This book is also dedicated to those who despite encountering difficult situations, make the most of life and empower others.*

Meva Singh Dhesi

# Reach for the

# Racquet

## The Sky's the Limit

Meyer & Meyer Sport

British Library of Cataloguing in Publication Data
A catalogue record for this book is available from the British Library


**Reach for the Racquet**
Maidenhead: Meyer & Meyer Sport (UK) Ltd., 2023
ISBN: 978-1-78255-242-0

© 2023 by Meyer & Meyer Sport (UK) Ltd.
Aachen, Auckland, Beirut, Cairo, Cape Town, Dubai, Hägendorf, Hong Kong, Indianapolis, Maidenhead, Manila, New Delhi, Singapore, Sydney, Tehran, Vienna

Member of the World Sport Publishers' Association (WSPA), www.w-s-p-a.org
Printed by Integrated Books International
Printed in the United States of America

ISBN: 978-1-78255-242-0
Email: info@m-m-sports.com
www.thesportspublisher.com

Photos: Courtesy of Alexander Ward, contact@alexward.photography; courtesy of Alan Spink https://actionphotography.photoshelter.com/index; and courtesy of Paul Parelka

# Contents

# FOREWORD

It is both a privilege and a pleasure to have been invited by Meva to write a foreword to his book. We have known each other for many years and have a shared joy in seeing disability badminton morph into a full-fledged Paralympic sport. However, it has not been without its hiccups and challenges along the way and there remain further opportunities for additional classifications and events to be embraced into future Paralympic Games. As Meva has illustrated throughout his book, one must have aspirations!

In addition to the sterling work and advocacy that Meva and many of his colleagues have put into spreading the word for the acceptance of badminton as being a sport in which many with disabilities can participate; much has also been done in parallel to aid inclusive badminton through the governance of the sport.

Throughout the period of my involvement with badminton for those with disabilities the governance of para-badminton has transited through being represented internationally by IBAD (the International Badminton Association for the Disabled) to become the PBWF (Para-Badminton World Federation), which eventually merged with the BWF (Badminton World Federation). It is with the backing of the BWF (the established and internationally recognised world governing body for the Olympic sport) that para-badminton finally gained acceptance as a Paralympic sport and was included in the Tokyo Paralympic Games in 2021.

The merger between the PBWF and the BWF was a happy coming together of knowledge, experience, commitment, and resources. It was this combination, plus greater knowledge and acceptance of badminton as being a sport in which those with disabilities could compete at a high level, which encouraged Member Associations of the BWF to embrace this aspect of badminton within their governance structures. This is now reflected in the fact that the membership of the Executive Board of the BWF includes a Vice-President for Para-Badminton, and the BWF Council now includes the Chair of the Para-Badminton Athletes' Commission in its membership. Whilst in some Member Associations, disability / para-badminton continues to have a National Disability Organisation as its governing body (often for very good reasons), I am pleased that in England, and many other nations, it is now embedded in the National Governing Body (NGB) for Badminton.

This embracing of disability / para-badminton has not been without its teething problems – often arising from a mixture of fears of the unknown and concerns about expectations. Even now I never tire of saying "see the ability, not the disability"!

Although para-badminton was not in the 2012 Paralympics in London, nevertheless that event did much to raise the profile and awareness of what could be achieved by those who had disabilities of one sort or another. Fortunately, the graphics which accompanied the televised events did much to explain the various classifications and events within them. This, I think, helped so much in embodying disability / para sports in the minds of so many across the world.

The first experience that my wife and I had working with athletes with disabilities stretches back some forty years at a multi-sports event, and we came away from that with feelings of both exhaustion and elation! This event was not intended for talented athletes but to give disabled young people the experience of the joy of sport and the social benefits that it could engender.

Many involved with able-bodied sport tend to think that, with rare exceptions, success at national / international level comes from young people following a "performance pathway", and largely that is true. However, one cannot approach disability / para sport with the same mind-set. True, some disabilities are present at birth or in early years, but so many others come to disability / para sport as a result of illness, accident or injury experienced much later in life – as in Meva's case. Often, prior to that life changing event, they have already experienced the joy of participation and success in sport as an able-bodied participant. The fact that life (and successful participation in sport) does not cease comes as a surprise and a challenge to many – as it did with Meva. However, he is not alone in having this experience and if this book does nothing else let us hope that it inspires others to engage or re-engage with sport (in our case, badminton!).

Only a very few years ago, nobody would have dreamt that a well-funded squad of four, internationally ranked, para-badminton players would be training full time with the goal of representing Great Britain at the Tokyo 2021 Paralympic Games. From years of dreams and aspirations it is so good to see how far we have advanced – nevertheless we must continue to "DREAM BIG! And aspire to even greater successes."

I wish Meva every success with his book and if it inspires you, do not delay, get involved NOW!

–Derek Batchelor

*Vice President, Badminton England*

# A Message of Support From Paul Kurzo

It is a great honour to be able to contribute to Meva's book. We have known each other for a long time dating back to 1995 when I played my first international tournament in Stoke Mandeville, England. I remember seeing this man with a turban chase the shuttlecock across the court. It was the first European Para-Badminton Championships and the birthplace of the International Badminton Association for the Disabled (IBAD). The 6 player countries that made up IBAD at the time were England, Germany, Israel, Switzerland, The Netherlands and Wales. Italy, the 7th country, initially took part in an observational capacity in an effort to learn how it worked.

My doubles partner that year was Jim Mackay and we finished third. You will read more about Jim later in the book. Unfortunately, Meva and I never played against each other as he was in the standing class, and I was in the wheelchair class. However, until my retirement at the World Championships 2005, we continued to see each other regularly at events. I have fond memories of many of the stories Meva recalls in this book. It was quite chaotic in the early days of para-badminton and we both saw the sport evolve with more players joining each year. We also saw it transform from a leisure activity to what it is today, a professional sport.

One thing that is special about the para-badminton community is the social interaction between the players. I remember we would have lengthy discussions as to how we could develop para-badminton and that one day we would hope to see it become a Paralympic sport.

Amazingly, some 20 years later, para-badminton will debut at the Tokyo 2021 Paralympic Games. While it is fantastic to see our vision come true, there is also a hint of regret that we were never able to participate at the Paralympics as players.

Meva, thank you for always being a good friend and companion. Your contribution to developing our beloved sport of para-badminton will always be treasured. I hope readers of this book enjoy your memories from the court.

–Paul Kurzo

*BWF Vice President for Para-Badminton and former player*

# A Message of Support From Richard Perot

I first met Meva, during the Spanish Para-Badminton International back in 2011. He was part of the English squad, a determined player and an obvious character!

As a new athlete in the para-badminton community, what amazed me was the cross-nation connection between players, and Meva was one of the first to welcome our newly founded French team into the "para-badminton family." Over the years and at different championships around the world I had the opportunity to have time with Meva where I discovered his charity activities and tireless strength to promote sport for the disabled. He has been really inspirational for me. He changed the way I see myself, being an international athlete, and the values I could carry.

Back in my country, it clearly pushed me and some of my team-mates to commit in a similar way. We decided to form FRAP (France Para-Badminton) of which I was, until today, the president. Later, following Meva's path, I was elected Chair of the newly created BWF Athletes' Commission.

We need people like Meva. I am so glad to have met him and I am sure there is a full generation of disabled young athletes he can inspire. Keep up the good job mate!

–Richard Perot

*BWF Chair, Para-Badminton Athletes' Commission*
*BWF Council Member*
*BWF Integrity Ambassador*
*IPC Agitos Foundation Proud Paralympian Educator*
*FRAP France Para-Badminton President*

*France National Paralympic Committee Ambassador*

# A Message of Support From Mike Robinson

Meva is a larger-than-life character. This book tells his amazing story from experiencing a horrific car accident to international success on the badminton court. Faced with a life changing event, this book tells how tenacity and a real determination to succeed can bring achievement, fulfilment, and great happiness.

Wishing you every success with the book.

–Mike Robinson

*Chair, Badminton England*

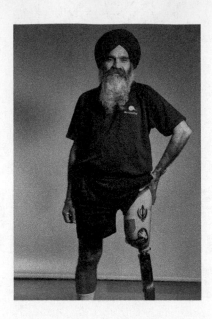

# Acknowledgements

I have really enjoyed writing about the sport I love: badminton. And more importantly, **Para-Badminton**. This book is a compilation of the incredible experiences and adventures that, knitted together over the years form the exciting tapestry of my life. To all the wonderful people who have influenced and supported me in my badminton efforts, I am truly grateful to you. I thank you for letting me mention you and share the stories of our para-badminton adventures within this book.

In those very early days of para-badminton there was no defined selection pathway for disabled players to show off their badminton skills by representing their country at the international level. The classification at that time was limited to above waist handicap, below waist handicap and wheelchair player. The degree of disability for wheelchair players was not broken down further for competition purposes. Of the 5 para-badminton players in the UK who wanted to compete at the highest levels possible, I was the only amputee on the team and was classified as having a below waist handicap.

As four standing players and one wheelchair player we took on the challenge to see how it would work out in the real world of international tournaments. We were self-selected and self-funded and felt like true pioneers for the sport of para-badminton at such a high level of competition. If an official Team GB (Paralympic) selection and funding process had been in place all those years ago, we would have been some of the first to apply and incredibly proud if we had been chosen to wear the official Team GB competition kit!

One person who truly deserves a special mention is Dr Jim Mackay; a Scottish wheelchair badminton player who made his home in Wales. He is a man with the vision, drive and energy to promote the concept of para-badminton as a competitive sport for UK players at the highest levels. He was convinced that it was possible, and that conviction gave us the motivation to make a sustained, consistent effort over many years to both play the sport and keep playing; to compete and keep competing locally, nationally and internationally.

Another inspirational, able-bodied player who I looked up to throughout my para-badminton career is Derek Batchelor. I met him when I started working with Badminton England developing the sport for other disabled players. From humble beginnings as a grassroots club player Derek went on to coach and develop the sport regionally and nationally. I invited him over to Germany to watch a para-badminton tournament, which he did. And he's been involved ever since.

So strong was his belief in the benefits of badminton / para-badminton that he rose through the ranks in various roles and went on to become Chairman of Badminton England for many years. Without his tremendous enthusiasm we wouldn't have achieved as much as we have as a nation within the sport. As recently as 2019 he handed over the honour of the Chairmanship to Michael Robinson who I am sure will do many great things in the role.

As para-badminton developed in the UK, so did the organisational and regulatory structures surrounding it. In the United Kingdom (UK) alone, an immense thank you must go to Badminton England, Badminton Scotland, Badminton Wales and to the Ulster Branch of Badminton Ireland for starting off the Four Nations competitions in particular. It's an excellent way for us to connect with our friends and fellow players around the UK.

In the very early days, (for amputees), para-badminton was simply one element of the Amputee Games organised annually by the British Amputee Sports Association. In later years they became the British Amputee Sports and Les Autres Association. The Amputee Games were always well supported every year by the Douglas Bader Foundation and often took place at Stoke Mandeville Stadium Leisure Centre, Aylesbury, England.

The International Badminton Association for the Disabled (IBAD) was eventually formed in 1995 at Stoke Mandeville. This was where the journey to include para-badminton within the Paralympics truly started. A special thanks goes to Paul Kurzo, Vice President for Para-Badminton at the BWF and Member of its Council and Executive Board for his kind assistance with this book. It is also important to mention Lyndon Williams who was Director of Badminton Wales and played a prominent role in expanding the para-badminton coach education and development programme globally. He was always there as a friend for me whenever I needed advice and a very helpful person who would go out of his way to assist and support badminton players as much as he possibly could. Also, thanks go to Richard Perot, France Para-Badminton President, BWF Chair, Para-Badminton Athletes' Commission, IPC Agitos Foundation Proud Paralympian Educator (amongst other roles). When I first met Richard, I found him to be very keen and we got on very well together. He has achieved the great heights of leadership in the sport which I dreamed of and aspired to when I was much younger.

The growth of para-badminton as a sport could not have taken place without the energetic participation of a long list of people at many different levels. All the players at local clubs, coaches, club members, umpires, tournament referees, organising committees, volunteers, line judges, tournament competitors and the countries hosting para-badminton tournaments around the world. You have created an exciting sports environment for us where we can truly flourish.

Way back in 1982, not long after I lost my leg, I was initially disappointed to learn that badminton wasn't in the Olympics/Paralympics. It was classed as a 'Demonstration Sport' for able-bodied players at the Olympic Games in Munich, Germany in 1972 so the badminton Olympic journey had started. But it took another twenty years before badminton for able bodied players officially became an Olympic Sport in Barcelona, Spain in 1992.

I didn't appreciate the situation regarding para-badminton and made up my mind to stick with the sport throughout all these years because I wanted to see it in the Paralympics. My dream was to help deliver that strong vision of people like Dr Jim Mackay from Wales, Derek Batchelor and others who were leading Badminton England at the time, and to do my best in as many ways as possible; playing, coaching, running a club and competing, in order to get para-badminton recognised as a sport within the Paralympics.

Of all the countries around the world that took on the spirit of the sport, a special thank you has to be given to The Netherlands. They really helped to lay those solid foundations that enabled para-badminton to be included within the Paralympics in 2020 due to be held in Tokyo. (Now delayed until 2021 due to the COVID19 global pandemic).

Competitive badminton at the international level is a tough and expensive sport. The companies that sponsored and supported my efforts throughout the years deserve a big thank you. For providing me with kit and equipment: Yonex, Carlton and Nicholas Goode, Managing Director of Goode Sport where I got my Ashaway badminton racquets. Thank you to the local newspapers for the promotional support over the years.

I thoroughly appreciate the kind generosity and friendship of the Totteridge Community, Sikh communities from North, South, West and East London, Sikh Role Model and Major Builders Merchants. You have all helped me to travel one step closer to my dream each time you donated to any of the causes for which I was fundraising. Thank you to Waheguru ji (God) for giving me the willpower and motivation to succeed.

Of course, if I had not been provided with prosthetic legs and medical support, my badminton career would have looked a little different. I would have been playing mostly out of a wheelchair rather than on two feet. I am tremendously grateful to Blatchford prosthetic manufacturers, and Stanmore Limb Centre NHS hospital staff for all their help.

A special thanks goes to Dr Linda J Marks, Consultant in Rehabilitation Medicine, a female consultant who gave 25 years of long service to the NHS at Stanmore Limb Centre before her retirement. Other medical staff that have been with me throughout my amputee life and helped me to overcome many issues include Dr Sedki, Professor Rajiv Hanspal and my numerous prosthetists, especially: H. Syed, Mark Croysdale and Emma Gillespie. More recently, I thank John Sullivan of Stanmore Limb Centre for my latest everyday leg with a Rheo XC microprocessor knee and a vacuum socket with Icecross silicone liner. The knee unit provides the all-important smart gait detection and real time data collection for smooth walking functionality. It's taken 3 years to get this new one but it's the perfect leg for me. Some of the delay was due to Covid 19 but without John Sullivan pushing hard to get me this leg I might still have been waiting another 3 or 4 years.

Now we are in 2022, I feel my own personal para-badminton journey is complete by writing this book. I am truly grateful to my whole family for all their support; particularly my wife, Kamalpreet Kaur Dhesi, for being there alongside me through everything over 44 years of marriage and blessing me with my children: Kirendeep Kaur Dhesi, Amandeep Kaur Dhillon, Herdeep Kaur Ward, Rubinder Kaur Dhesi and Birinder Singh Dhesi. I am also grateful to my sons- in- law, Harpinder Singh Dhillon and Benjamin Singh Ward and my grandchildren. They have enriched my life outside badminton immeasurably.

Thank you as well to all the people who, in one way or another, have contributed to making it possible for me to have my life documented within this book and especially my sponsors: Blatchford Prosthetics Suppliers; Larry Wood, Managing Director at Hummingbird Kia in Colindale, London; Satnam Singh Maan, Managing Director, Major Builders Merchants in Ilford, Essex; Amritpal Singh Maan, Managing Director, of Punjab Restaurant, Covent Garden, London and Dr Zak Pallikaros, Managing Director of Pumping Iron Gym, London N11. Thanks also to the photographers Alexander Ward, Alan Spink and Paul Parelka, web designer Benjamin Singh Ward and Jatinder Palaha for IT and web support.

Thank you finally to my editor, Sonia Sanghani, who has worked closely with me on this idea. It's been a pleasure to create something so wonderful together. Even though I didn't believe her when she told me it would take us at least 4 years and maybe longer to complete. This could only have been possible with the generous support of Martin Meyer and Liz Evans of Meyer and Meyer Sport who offered to publish this book and patiently worked with Sonia and me to produce the final product. This book is unique. Truly one of a kind. And I hope it inspires many generations of para-badminton players with any disability in years to come.

Whilst this book is autobiographical it's not easy to remember everything so clearly after all these years. So I have granted myself a little bit of artistic license during the writing process. I'm sure you'll still enjoy it and I hope it interests you enough to support para-badminton players who are competing for your region or your country. Or, even better, take up the sport yourself. If there is one thing I'd like to leave you with it's this. In life, be a fighter. Be determined. Set yourself a target and try to achieve it. Go for it. Expect there to be many hurdles along the way which you will be required to overcome. You will get there if you really want to.

**When you have read this book, please feel free to connect with me via:**

     *www.mevasinghdhesi.uk*

     *www.facebook.com/people/Meva-Singh-Dhesi/100000306056590*

Let me know what you think of my book. If it interests you in learning more about badminton and / or para-badminton it will be my pleasure to help guide you.

# 2<sup>nd</sup> July 1980

*An ordinary day in the summer of 1980.*

*A July day. Just like any other. But it wasn't.*

*It started off exactly the same but ended up being dramatic, painful and life changing.*

*Every second of **that day** burned deep into my memory, tearing at my soul. Never allowing me to forget.*

*You don't appreciate what you have. Until you lose it!*

*It's a cliché that resonates deep within me each time I look back on **that day**.*

*I lost something so precious; so fundamental to my being that at the time, I didn't know how I was ever going to survive without it.*

*I was the breadwinner, the man of the family, the one they all relied on.*

*How on earth could this happen to me? And why did it have to happen now?*

# Chapter 1
# There's a Big Scratch on It Now!

The minicab office was on the 2nd floor (with no lift) in North Finchley High Road. I'd done a few local jobs that day and my knee was starting to bother me. Stomping grumpily downstairs, I dragged myself out into the searing hot afternoon sun reflecting harshly off the hard concrete pavement. Neatly side stepping the chewing gum that almost caught me earlier I headed morosely to the car.

North Finchley High Road is full of small retailers and restaurants and the warm weather brought out the shoppers. Post Offices, butchers, tailors, greengrocers and dry cleaners were eagerly looking forward to a busy few hours before they closed for the night. Theirs was an elegant rhythm that had played on the street for decades. Shops would unfurl their awnings made of plain coloured, hard-wearing fabrics, stretching over well-dressed windows in the morning and roll them back in the evening through boom times, recessions, closures, new owners and more. I'm quite sure if the shops, pubs and restaurants of North Finchley High Road could talk they would have some fascinating stories to tell of life throughout the years.

I reached my car, a brand-new Mitsubishi Gallant, which was parked right opposite the taxi office in between two bus stops on the one-way system. I was parked facing north going towards Barnet. There was no central locking in cars in those days. It was all manual key entry, manual window roll up and down and certainly no satellite navigation systems. We learnt the roads and found our way. Talking of cars, I've always had a Mitsubishi. I'd never buy anything else. Mitsubishi are known for their reliability and good engines. They always start without any problem and don't let you down. I always buy my cars from the same dealership, Humming Bird Motors, not far from where I live. They are a family run company that have been running the dealership for 4 generations and the current managing director is Larry Wood. This was my second car, a nice brown Mitsubishi Gallant. I've had lots of cars since then in all different colours. The blue version was my favourite but now I've got a white one and a silver one. Who knows, one day I might just take the plunge and go for my dream car; a Jaguar.

As I put the key in the lock to open the door I heard a loud BANG followed by an ear-splitting screeching of brakes. My left leg was behind me and my right leg was leaning in towards my car. Looking round I saw an out-of-control vehicle swerving straight towards me! It hit me squarely in the left leg, twisted me over and dragged me along to the front wheel arch of my car before finally coming to a stop. Although it took only a minute or two, I could see and feel it all in slow motion. It was like I was watching it all from above and it was happening to someone else. Not me. There was a lady driver at the wheel and she was visibly upset. I just caught her eye and the panicked expression on her face as I turned round to see her car behaving like a crazed steel lion careering wildly in my direction; growling fiercely at everyone in the area. Right before it smashed into me.

Panicked passers-by and shoppers all started running towards us to help. As I lay on the ground trying to comprehend what had just happened to me, I could hear scared voices. Faces, lots of faces, blurring in and out of focus, everywhere I looked. Screaming. Shouting. Concerned and chaotic,

*'Quick, call the police and ambulance,' they shouted to each other.*

*'Don' move 'im, y'musen' move 'im.'*

*'Oh my Gawd, there's blood, oh I don't like blood.*

I was fully conscious and in a terrific amount of pain. It was sheer agony and terrifying at the same time. All I could see was my left leg lying there in front of me, totally twisted; literally smashed up and hanging off below the knee. Blood was pouring out of it, gushing and squirting everywhere. Because of the lovely hot weather, I was wearing a nice new T-shirt. It was now splattered with blood but, strangely enough, the only thing I could think about was:

*'b..... hell my brand new car's got damaged - there's a big scratch on it now.'*

Which goes to show what my priorities in life were at the time.

Before long I heard the sirens of the police and ambulance vehicles and started to breathe a little easier. Someone had actually managed to get through to the emergency services after all. Hopefully they would be able to sort out the situation, and more than anything else, get me out of pain. *So much pain.* It was all I could feel. *Searing. Burning. Pain.* I lay there uncomfortably on that hot tarmac road watching it melt in front of me, fading in and out as I battled to stay conscious.

North Finchley High Road is wide enough to allow two cars to pass even if there is a bus parked on the side. In those days the bus stops were just two small round metal painted signs saying 'bus stop' on thin grey steel posts. No bus shelters, no seats, no information boards with timetables on them or red or yellow lines on the road. The white bus stop sign was for the normal red buses of London Transport and the other bus stop was for the Green Line buses of Hertfordshire.

Around this time in the afternoon, school buses would pick children up from Ballard's Lane stop just around the corner from the High Street. They would come out from St Michael's Catholic Girls' School in Nether Street and stroll over in groups or pairs to catch the bus home. You'd often see them all gather around the pavement chatting, giggling, or hopping on the bus excitedly waving to their friends. The girls that lived closest to the school would sometimes hang around, look into the shop windows, or head over to Victoria Park to play in the fresh air after all those lessons indoors on such a hot day. Had the accident happened just a few minutes later the driver of the car that hit me would have ploughed into the children waiting for the bus. So it could have all ended up a lot worse than it did.

The ambulance wasn't far behind the police and they got straight to work strapping up the leg and getting me into the vehicle. As we left for the hospital, the ambulance crew tried to make me feel better by saying,

*'it's alright mate, it's only a scratch,'*

but I knew it was a bit more serious than that. As they sped me through the busy roads to the hospital my thoughts wandered back to the minicab office and the customer pick up that I'd left behind.......

It was 3:15pm on the day of the accident and we were in the drivers' sitting room of the minicab offices. The mid-afternoon sun streamed through the narrow single pane window and warmed my back. The steady hum of traffic and sounds of everyday life in North Finchley High Road filtered distantly through the glass creating that all familiar buzz around me. It was the balmy hot summer of 1980 and the final tense deciding matches of Wimbledon.

*'15 all. Second serve. Quiet please,'* said the umpire as the players got ready for the next point. The commentators, John Barrett, Dan Maskell and Mark Cox had a way with words that literally drew me inside the television screen. It was a small Phillips colour TV with just 3 channels to choose from; BBC1, BBC2 and ITV. Even then, I felt I had melted right into the heart of the excited crowd.

Tennis was dominated by the Borg v McEnroe story that year. It was McEnroe's first Wimbledon final. The crowd had an early glimpse into his firecracker temper during the semi-final against Jimmy Connors. They booed really loudly when he entered the court for the final against Borg who was defending his title as Wimbledon champion for the 5th year. Not that any of it put McEnroe off. Even though Borg eventually beat him, the exciting hard fought fourth set tie break won by McEnroe was a masterpiece of tennis. Something that still gets mentioned amongst tennis players and fans 40 years later. That year, Martina Navratilova reached the semi-finals. Little did we know then that Borg would soon retire from competitions at the tender age of 26 and that Navratilova would go on to win Wimbledon *9 times*. All in the space of a few short years.

As I sat there my mind started to drift lazily into a comfortable haze. The picture of crisp green tennis lawns softly melted away. In its place were the indoor courts of the All England Badminton Championships at Wembley Arena. In my mind I heard Dan Maskell's gentle voice saying his signature expressions, *'Oh I say,' 'quite extraordinary' and 'dream of a backhand,'* as Gillian Gilks and Nora Perry won the women's badminton doubles. Nora Perry and Mike Tredgett went on to win the mixed doubles and the men's doubles saw England come in as runners up that year. I dreamt that the great TV and radio commentators were celebrating my badminton heroes to packed audiences and houses around the country. Badminton was much more exciting and fast paced than tennis as far as I was concerned. It was easily 'up there' with football and cricket. Just as I was revelling in my fellow badminton players winning trophies in front of imaginary cheering crowds of spectators, the 'phone rang.

*'Hey, Meva - your customer - nice lady from this morning. Wants you to pick her up from the Royal Free Hospital and take her back to Barnet,'* said the boss cheerfully as he put down the receiver.

He was always cheerful when he had customers and very grumpy when there weren't any. It was a money thing. My boss was a handsome, friendly, middle aged Greek Cypriot who treated me well. We sort of had something in common because Cyprus used to be a British colony (just like India) until it's very recent independence in 1960. The unrest between Greeks and Turks on the island following independence led many of them to come to London in search of safety and prosperity. It reminded me a lot of the 1947 Indian Independence struggle and the partition of India and Pakistan. History seems to have a way of repeating itself I thought at the time. Not much seems to have changed around the world since. So many decades later there are still similar struggles. They are just in different locations.

*'Boss mate, I don't want to pick her up, just waiting for my wife to ring and go home. Shift's nearly over now.'*

My main job was driving London transport buses. My wife, Kamalpreet Kaur and I were trying to save up to buy our own house so we could start a family. Prices in London, around Finchley and Barnet especially, were fairly high and we knew we would both have to work hard. So I also drove minicabs part time. I had just been off work for nearly 4 weeks because of a cartilage operation on my knee. Following the medical all clear, I had given London Transport notice that I could come back to work on the buses next week. The shorter mini cab shifts were a way of easing myself into it all again.

My wife worked in Barnet, and going to do this extra pick up at the Royal Free would mean I'd be late meeting her. But the customer had asked for me in particular. I'd dropped her off at the Royal Free in the morning. She knew me and asked specifically for me because I had a nice new car with a brand-new stereo system in it. Just that morning we'd been talking about how 'Crying' by Don McLean was in its 3rd week at the top of the charts. Songs all sounded so much better with the speaker system in the Gallant. Whenever I drove my customers anywhere I made an effort to chat with them. We'd discuss all sorts of things; traffic, weather, family, work, politics and anything else that they had on their minds. Happy things, sad things, anything. Putting that little bit of effort in usually meant they would ask for me in person next time they needed a taxi.

I had to ask the police officer who came to check on me at the accident site to get the keys out of the driver's door of my car and take them back to the taxi office. So my boss knew what was going on and could send another driver to pick up my customer. I'm sure my boss was thinking 'that's one hell of a way of trying to get out of a taxi job, Meva!' but I'm glad we can laugh about what happened now.

He arranged for someone else to do my call once he'd got over the shock of seeing the police bring my keys into his office. My wife had simply come home by bus totally unaware that I was in hospital. We had a bit of a neat arrangement. If my car was parked outside her workplace when she finished then I was picking her up. If it wasn't, she made her way home by bus.

There were no mobiles in those days with which to text each other, only the old style 'phones in the house where the handset was attached by a plastic cord to the main 'phone. Whenever we needed to ring anyone we'd have to use the round dial with our fingers and dial the letters first, then the numbers, such as Fin 346.

The other alternative was the red public telephone boxes in the street where you put in money. Well, as you can imagine, I was in no fit state to ring anyone as I was a bit busy bleeding profusely in the middle of North Finchley High Road at that particular point in time. So she thought nothing of it when I wasn't there waiting to pick her up that day. It was only as she put the key in the door and walked into the house at 5.30pm, a whole TWO HOURS after my accident that she found out what had happened to me.

As she entered the living room she could hear my mum crying and upset. She went to find out what the problem was, thinking it was something that my dad had done (again!) or some upsetting news from India or something like that. Little did she think that when she walked in, and asked what the matter was, they would sit her down to tell her the police had just been to the house. To tell them that Meva, her husband, had been injured in an accident.

The police didn't have to come very far to see us. Their living quarters were only two doors away from our house. So they knew me and my family pretty well. My father had actually been in the area that afternoon and heard the commotion. He asked passers-by what was going on and someone said a young boy had been taken to hospital in the ambulance. He didn't think it was anyone he knew. It was only when the police came later on with the bad news that he realized.

My wife froze in shock when they told her. Almost feeling as if she wasn't really there. My parents' anxious, upset voices faded in and out painfully around her. Jumbled up, tumbling around and repeating over and over again.

*'Meva......accident.....badly injured.....Barnet hospital.'*

Over and over in her head the words kept circling, making her feel faint, numb and giddy.

*'Surely they meant someone else? They'd got it wrong,'* she thought, trying to fight her way through the dense, dark fog of emotions whirling mercilessly around her, gripping her tightly in strangled panic and fear.

*'It couldn't be true because Meva was a safe and careful driver. He drove buses and taxis for goodness sake so he couldn't have had an accident. He was a responsible driver who looked after others. No, it simply wasn't true,'* she cried inwardly.

*'It's a mistake and Meva's alright. They've got him mixed up with someone else perhaps. These things happen don't they?'* she said to my parents again and again, still refusing to believe what they had just told her.

*'And if it was true? If he had been in an accident? Then it couldn't have been his fault. He would be okay.'* she mumbled incoherently as the shock of the news finally started to sink in.

*He would be okay, she would make sure he'd be okay. Oh dear God, he would be okay, wouldn't he?*

It slowly dawned on her that the sickening drama unfolding before her was true. She made a supreme effort to shake herself out of her thoughts and try to figure out what to do next. With a trembling hand she brushed aside the endless stream of tears that threatened not to stop flowing down her face. Hot, salty, wet tears, under her chin and through the collar of the work uniform that she'd still not had a chance to change out of.

*'C-can we, g-go, t-to the hospital, t-t-to see how he is?'* she hiccoughed and gulped. *'I really need to be with him to make sure he's okay.'*

It was a major shock to the three people I cared most about in all my life and they had no idea as to the extent of the injuries I had received. There was no-one with a car around and I was the only driver in the house so they decided to catch the bus to Barnet General Hospital. It was a long and stressful journey for them because at each stop people would get on and off and that all took time. Time that they didn't want to spend on a bus. Time that they would rather spend with me.

I had been taken to Barnet General Hospital earlier in the afternoon, fully conscious and in a lot of pain despite the painkillers. Hot burning waves went searing right through me with every sharp twist and turn the ambulance took through the streets, flashing its blue lights and blaring sirens loudly in order to get me there quickly. When we got to the casualty ward staff asked me, *'what's your name, address, date of birth and what have you had to eat?'*

The strong painkillers the ambulance crew had given me were starting to finally kick in. I was getting that 'woozy drugged up' feeling so my answers were coming out very slurred; like I'd been drinking heavily or had been punched in the face during a brawl at a football match.

*'tdwoo backet cwishpsh an' coackha colha'* (2 packets of crisps and Coca Cola)

Which meant they couldn't operate on the leg until much later that night. When my wife and parents finally got to Barnet General Hospital I was in the casualty ward. All drugged up and unaware of what was going on around me. There were a lot of tears shed and everyone was so upset but also relieved to see that I was at least alive. In the next 4 weeks my wife lost over 2 stone in weight with the shock and stress of it all. The doctors did their best to try to save the leg but there was no circulation and it started going black. On Friday they asked my parents if it was okay to cut the leg off. My mum was devastated; crying and worrying about it but I said,

*'Look I still have my brain and my hands and there's been no other damage.'*

So they cut my left leg off above the knee. I spent the next two weeks on strong medication coming to terms with not having a leg anymore. Continuously drugged up. Totally out of it. Sleeping. No clue what was going on around me. I was really upset when I finally realised what it meant to be without a leg.

I found there were so many things that I simply couldn't 'just get up and do' like I used to. For those first few weeks I was so helpless, heavily reliant on the nurses and medical teams to make me feel better. My whole life was upside down. The whole of my family had their world turned inside out too. When you're lying there in a hospital bed, even when there are other patients on the ward, you feel sad and lonely inside because you're only allowed to see the people you love during visiting times. Outside the hospital, in your everyday life, you're used to having the people you love around you from the moment you wake up to the time you go to sleep. And it's when you're in hospital going through a life changing experience that you feel you need them most. By your side, going through everything with you.

It can get quite monotonous if you are in hospital for a long time. Once you start feeling a bit better, but have to stay in a restricted state, just lying there in the bed, you get bored, depressed and angry. The days stretch out forever in front of you interrupted only for mealtimes, medication rounds and visiting times.

At 6am every morning the nurses would come round with tea and breakfast. At 8am they would change over staff, and from 9am they'd start making the beds and giving patients bed baths. It was the middle of a hot summer so the daylight hours were at their longest. All my waking hours I would be thinking about how everyone was getting on at the badminton club and whether I'd ever be able to join in with them again.

The sun would come streaming in through the big windows and heat up the whole ward. It felt hot and stuffy a lot of the time and the sheets would get very sweaty. The heat would make the pain around my stump really uncomfortable whilst it was bandaged up and the sweating would make it itchy and irritating. At my worst moments it felt like being in prison because I literally couldn't go anywhere until I was well enough to use the ward wheelchair.

It was only in the third week, when they were fully satisfied that everything was working as it should, that they moved me along to the recovery ward. It was such a relief when they did because it signified to me and my family that I was getting better and it wouldn't be too long before I was out of hospital and back home with them.

That week I asked if I could get out of bed and help the nurses make tea for everyone in my old ward. I was in a wheelchair by this time and had been moved the previous night into the recovery ward. I took a patient a cup of tea. He was screaming and in a lot of pain. Looking closer I saw it was actually one of the guys I had worked with at the greengrocers, which is what I used to do before I started driving buses and taxis. He had been admitted following a motorbike accident and had broken both his legs. I stayed and chatted to him to help him through it as best I could whilst I was there. Luckily his injuries healed up quite well so they didn't have to amputate any of his limbs.

It was far different for another patient on the same ward. There were at least 40 patients in a very long ward split into two halves so there was always lots going on all around us. This particular patient had been in hospital for about 6 months after his motorcycle accident. His leg was in a stretcher because they were waiting for everything to knit back properly after putting a metal plate in his knee.

He was a youngster, around 19 years of age. Even though he was the one riding the motorcycle he kept taking everything out on his parents, refusing to talk to them when they came to visit. He was constantly moaning and groaning all through the day about his situation. It certainly made me and my friend realise how lucky we both were as our prospects for getting out of hospital after only a few short weeks made the whole experience more bearable. Even though I had lost a leg in the process, it was still better than being that youngster.

There was a television in the recovery ward and one day it was showing the results of the Paralympics. That was where I saw a one-legged man doing the high jump. After seeing something as amazing as that, I kept wondering what other sports could be done without a leg? Could I too reach for the sky as he had, I asked myself? It really changed the way I thought about losing my leg. Watching someone with the same issue as I, do something so extraordinary was a real tonic. It helped get me out of the negative spiral of emotions that were crowding around my head following the accident.

I'd spend most of the time thinking about my family, my friends and badminton. Would I be able to play again? How would I feel about depending on my family to look after me? It made me feel really guilty even thinking about how much I was putting them through already, whilst in hospital, that I couldn't even begin to imagine what life would be like once I got out. It was such a stressful time for all of us. Luckily I was able to talk about it with my family and friends whilst I was going through it. They wanted me to tell them how I was feeling, what I was thinking and to help me work out how we were going to cope with everything now I had no left leg.

One day, in an effort to cheer me up, my friends brought over some watermelon and other tasty sweet summer fruits and asked the nurses if they could take my bed out into the courtyard.

*'cos Meva needs to do a bit of sunbathing. He's looking a bit pale and we'd like to give him a picnic outside,'* they said cheekily.

They allowed my friends to wheel my bed out into the fresh air and sunshine away from the smell of detergents and hospital food. We told each other some jokes, caught up on all the latest news and ate some sweet summer fruits together. Other patients on my ward started to join us in their wheelchairs and beds too. It was such a good atmosphere and just the nicest thing that they could have done to help me feel better.

I got on well with the nurses. The matron and the ward sister, Sister Buck, were the best as they always permitted me more visitors. Usually, it's only 2 people allowed at a time during visiting hours. All my friends from the greengrocers would visit me and bring far more fruit than I could eat so I'd give the extra fruit to the nurses. Nurses and patients don't usually mix after leaving hospital but I ended up being a really good friend with the ward sister for many years after I left the hospital. I even went to Sister Buck's husband's funeral. I used to ring them and visit them sometimes. They were always there for me.

Having friends, family and work colleagues visit you really helps when recovering from something as traumatic as losing a leg. There were so many cards with lovely messages on them like these:

*'on behalf of all your friends at Gainsborough - we look forward to seeing you soon, love and best wishes'*

*'get well soon'*

*'frightened of next year's competition - good luck'*

*'some of your Hadley friends'*

When they came to see me I'd chat about life in the hospital and how the medication gave me funny thoughts and dreams. It's probably where I started dreaming about playing badminton in the Paralympics one day in the future. On July 31st, my badminton friends from the clubs put some money together to buy me a small portable JVC TV/radio/cassette (3 in1) with a 5-inch screen. They told me to use that instead of going to watch the main TV in the ward so I could just tune into whatever I wanted. It was a very touching gesture and really helped motivate me to get better. I was discharged just a week later.

## ∼ Smelly Socks Are Good for Smuggling Cigarettes ∼

Before my accident, my first experience of a badminton competition outside England was in Guernsey. I wasn't wearing a turban at the time so I looked like an average clean shaven young man. We flew from Bournemouth Airport over to Guernsey. My team-mates drank and smoked so they wanted to get lots of duty-free on the way back for themselves, friends or family members. I didn't drink alcohol or smoke so my duty-free allowance was something they really wanted. Otherwise, they would have been fined at the Customs checkpoint and the extra goods confiscated. I wasn't too keen on the idea of putting such items in my luggage but agreed because it's what friends do for each other. The only problem was that actually all of us were well over the limit allowed so we would have been in big trouble if we were stopped and searched.

Badminton is a tough game and everything from socks to underwear to shorts and t-shirts all get really sweaty and smelly. Add to that a couple of days of not washing the clothes and leaving them locked in a small holdall, the whole shebang can get really stinky!

We'd just got off the airplane on our return journey and were heading for the green "Nothing to Declare" exit when the Customs official asked me to come over and show him my bag. Just my luck, I thought. I didn't want him to open the holdall and look too closely inside as I knew I had too much duty-free in there. As I walked over to the Customs table I was inwardly fuming and cursing the other guys for putting me in such a situation. The Customs official asked for my key. As I slapped it down hard on the table I put a mean scowl on my face, looked him straight in the eye and in my deepest voice said to him:

*'Here's the key. If you open it, you lock it properly again. 'Cos I'm not doing it.'*

Customs officials obviously come across a lot of aggressive people in their job so he didn't bat an eyelid at the way I said that to him. He calmly took the key from the table and opened the case. As he did, all my dirty, sweaty badminton clothes and socks fell out and he backed away, grimacing ferociously at the stink. It really was a foul smell and thinking back it was totally embarrassing but it did the trick! He quickly stuffed all the dirty clothes into the holdall, whilst trying not to retch and be sick, and let me go.

I certainly wasn't going to argue with his judgement on that. I calmly walked out of the door, doing my best not to look too smug at having got the better of him, and looked around to find everyone else. They were all waiting in a taxi for me so I jumped in trying not to pump my fist in the air, dance a jig or anything that would give the game away and make him call me back. The whole affair with that Customs official put us an hour behind schedule so to make up for that the guys I was travelling with paid my taxi fare home. The success of that haul wasn't quite enough to turn me into an international cigarette and alcohol smuggler, though, which, on balance, is a good thing I guess.

## ∽ SNAP! We Concede, They Win! ∽

My first Flying Feathers men's doubles handicap club tournament following the loss of my leg took place at the Orion Hall, Stamford Hill in 1985. I was playing in clubs where the players were all able bodied, the only amputee amongst 80 or 90 clubs in the surrounding area. I had trained hard for this opportunity to compete against the able-bodied badminton players in my club and was really looking forward to it.

The event turned out to be exciting and soul destroying all at the same time. The Orion Hall is an imposing building with very high ceilings, dark wooden floors and dark green walls inside. The wood used for the flooring has a certain amount of 'springiness.' It's good for playing badminton as it gives and bounces back as you step on it (the structure under the floor does that). There's even a stage at one side of the hall but from the outside it just looks very old and a bit of a tip. It was always occupied in the evenings by different clubs. A lot of international badminton players had competed there over the years so you felt as though you were in a hallowed place. It really meant something to be there that day. The Orion Hall was one of the original badminton halls before sports centres came along. There was no money for refurbishment, so the owners sold it. The new owners wanted to knock it down entirely and build houses there. As it turned out, they didn't get planning permission so now it's just used for warehouse storage instead.

There we were, my doubles partner Ian Montgomery and I, competing in the semi-final. Ian was around 5'8" / 5'9", slim, fit, had light coloured hair and always wore sports glasses. This was in the days before contact lenses. He was a member of the Flying Feathers and one of the top players in our club. He was so good at badminton that he was playing handicapped tournaments. This is where the top seeded players give away points to their opponents at the start. He was a very determined player. Consistent and cool and it was very rare that you'd see him lose his temper in a match. He would always give me lots of encouragement to play more even though I lost my leg and was negatively handicapped in scoring, which meant that other players used to give me points at the start. He lives in Scotland now but we are still in touch.

We were at a tense moment in the match, really close to getting through to the final. The scoring went up to 15 points only at that time and we were already 14-all. We only needed that last point. One. Point. Just one. Nothing more. Surely that wasn't asking for much was it? Ian served and the receiver returned with a clever drop shot that skimmed close to the net. Luckily for us, I was standing at the front of the court and reached forward to meet it. It was only just high enough for me to slice deftly with my backhand, and I watched it expectantly as it glided gracefully over the net to give us the winning point.

It was a match I absolutely wanted to win so my nerves were already on edge. I finished the shot by landing on my prosthetic leg as I completed my follow through. Suddenly, out of nowhere, I heard a sharp,

'SNAP,'

and a strange cracking noise like a single barrel shotgun going off. I felt the prosthetic hit my normal flesh and remaining leg bone. This version of prosthetic had a hinge mechanism with a pin. I hadn't been given a suspension sleeve to wear in those days, so the socket was held on with a belt strap and harness. *And right at that moment, at the most tense part of the semi-final, the pin* **SNAPPED**.

I was mortified. Couldn't believe it! We were through to the FINAL. In my first ever club tournament following the loss of my leg. And this happens! Ian heard the noise too. He came over looking very concerned as I lay on the floor staring incredulously at my leg and asked,

*'Should we go on playing Meva?'*

I was really upset and told him that my prosthetic leg had broken and couldn't be fixed easily. Although we won this match I wouldn't be able to play in the finals as the leg would have to come off and I didn't have a spare one. So he made the tough decision to concede to our opponents. They came up to me as I sat there on the floor in disbelief and shook my hand. I was so upset that I actually started crying and saying things like,

*'We'll never get into the final again.'*

Ian was quite touched that I felt so strongly about winning the match with him that he smiled and told me gently not to be silly.

*'There will be more finals ahead for you, Meva.'*

And he was right. There were. And I made sure that I won them too!

## ～ Don't Sympathise, You Might Lose? ～

Mill Hill Church Hall was the venue for the Middlesex Men's 6 Badminton League matches. My club (Hadley) was playing against the All Saints. Charlie Chogley and I were partnered together having the best time of our lives. I was still getting used to wearing my left prosthetic leg for hours a day as well as doing sharp twists, dives, turns and short bursts of running in different directions on the badminton court. We would start the matches around 7pm in the evening and often carry on playing until well past the official closing time of 11pm. Sometimes it would be midnight before we locked up. We had a key to the hall so we could play longer if we needed to. It's not possible to carry on playing so late in leisure centres nowadays.

In 1980's badminton, the best of 3 games was known as a rubber (match) and each game was played to 15 points. Points were only given if the server won the rally. Charlie and I had lost our first rubber 1:2 against the All Saints, so we were feeling a bit disheartened because we had expected to win it. I was still using the metal Mappe leg at the time. When I play badminton I always lock the knee and play with a stiff leg. This knee wasn't computerised like the later ones that I had in 1992.

We were now in the 2nd game of the 2nd rubber and our All Saints opponents weren't taking it easy on us. It was a tough one. We had lost the first game and were winning the second game. It was the most exciting phase of the match with everything to play for. Charlie and I were determined to fight back and win when, in the middle of the game, the waistband snapped and the leg broke again!

*'Oh no, not again Meva? Seriously?'* shouted Charlie, looking at me incredulously as I stumbled head first inelegantly onto the floor with a twisted leg splayed out behind me, the foot facing the wrong way entirely.

*'B..... hell, I don't believe it! This waistband is absolutely useless. Damn it! My other leg is at home, not in my car. I feel like such a fool, I only took it out of the boot 2 days ago!'* I groaned back to Charlie, cursing myself inwardly for being so disorganised.

The All Saints players had rushed across to see what the problem was and heard what I had said.

*'It's okay, Meva. Don't fret. What's the best way to get your spare leg? Can one of us drive you home to get it?'* one asked.

*'Nice tactic Meva, wish I had a prosthetic leg like yours which kept breaking. You were making this second game hard work for us. I'll be glad of the rest until you get your spare!'* laughed his partner, winking at me.

*'Sure you don't want me to drive you back to the house, Meva?'* asked Charlie, still looking concerned. *'I'd really like to help you if I can.'*

*'Ugh, should be okay, thanks mate,'*

I shrugged, struggling to my feet and checking whether my stump would stay in place well enough to get to the car at least. I secured the prosthetic on as tight as I could using some thick weave cotton socks, wiggled everything about a bit and announced

*'I'll go and get the spare. I've an automatic so won't need my left leg to drive anyway.'*

That settled, the other players from both teams all agreed to carry on playing their rubbers whilst I went to fetch my spare leg. I looked an absolute sight as I left the hall, dragging my left leg behind me and bending over, using both hands to keep the leg in position going down the steps outside. Otherwise, it would have fallen off and I would have face-planted on the concrete next to it! Luckily the car was close to the entrance, and I hopped in quickly, adrenaline pumping. Half out of embarrassment that this had happened in a match and half out of excitement that at least we had been given the chance to carry on playing. *If I could only get my spare leg.*

I drove as fast as I possibly could, every traffic light conspiring to turn red just as I reached it. A learner driver ahead - go on, turn left, turn left so I can get past you! Now a bus, why wasn't it using the bus lane? No wonder, parked cars in the way! Why was everyone driving so slowly, what were they doing out at this time of night anyway! Curfew, that's what slow drivers need. Or was it just because I was speeding that I thought everyone else was going slow and getting in the way?

I kept looking at my mirror to double check that there were no police cars following behind me and swerved quickly into the parking spot right outside my shop. I made my way up the stairs holding the prosthetic leg with both hands, hobbling up each step and leaning against the wall for support to keep me balanced. I grabbed my spare leg from the bedroom and hobbled back downstairs, jumped into the car and drove like the devil back to the hall. I must have been gone for nearly 25 minutes or more. I'm sure they thought I only lived around the corner in Finchley. I hadn't mentioned that I was now living above the shop in East Barnet which was at least 3 miles away!

Unfortunately for Charlie he had to sit on the side and just watch everyone else compete whilst I went to get my leg which must have seemed boring, I guess. At least he could report back all the action to me from our team-mates as I changed legs but he was a bit worried that he had cooled down too much to play as well as earlier in the evening.

*'You'll be fine Charlie mate. We were winning the game just before my leg broke, remember? And your shots are bang on target, outclassing them easily'*

I said encouragingly, a bit out of breath after all that racing around. If such a thing had happened nowadays, I would have simply used my mobile phone to ring my wife or one of my children to drop the spare leg over to me but it wasn't an option then.

As we headed to the court, All Saints were winning 4:3 overall. Luckily, my spare leg fitted me well so playing badminton wasn't too difficult with it on. It took me a point or two to get back into the rhythm of it and we won the game which put us at 1:1. Charlie and I went all out to win the next game in style to seal the rubber 2:1. If our opponents hadn't been kind enough to let me get my spare leg then we would have had to concede the rubber. We would have been out of the match, sidelined and sent home, or just watching our team-mates play instead of us.

The overall score was now 4:4 and it couldn't have been more exciting at this stage for both teams. A lot of players had finished playing their rubbers and started to pack up and head off home but Charlie and I still had our final rubber to play. Not only were we tired by that time, we were also under more pressure because of the 4:4 score. The tension was swirling all around us as we headed to the court for the very last rubber of the night.

We must have been on an adrenaline high because we went on to win with another score of 2:1 which meant Hadley beat the All Saints 5:4 in that match. Over the moon? You bet we were! The sympathy and kindness they showed me on court that evening meant All Saints lost, but they will always be winners in my heart.

## ∼ It Was OUT! ∼

We were playing a para-badminton tournament in Spain and things weren't going too well for me. I was up against Gustaav Maasen (Guus), a player from The Netherlands and it was very tight between us. I won the first game but he came back sharply and won the second game. That meant we had to play a third game. Playing against him was tense and exhilarating at the same time. I was winning my points because my forehand sliced cross-court drop shots were a dream and right on target. No matter what he tried, he couldn't return them so took points off me by directing shots to my backhand which was my weaker area. It was really tiring and the pressure was building for both of us with each point. We were now 19:19 in the third game (the scoring system now having been changed to the best of 3 games to 21 points).

In the next rally he returned my shot and the shuttle whizzed past my racquet and landed wide of the court markings. Obviously I was expecting the score to be 20:19 to me. You can imagine my disbelief when the linesman called

*'Out'*

and the umpire announced they had given the point to my opponent, Guus! Naturally, without a doubt and no hesitation I had to dispute it; the shot had gone out as far as I was concerned. In accordance with the laws of badminton the game was stopped, the referee came over and we explained the issue. He listened and after some consideration, said

*'The umpire's decision is final and you have to accept it, Play on.'*

Was I fuming? You bet I was! I was ab-sol-ute-ly livid. Ready to erupt like a volcano, like a whole row of volcanoes in fact. But we went back on court to continue playing as instructed by the referee and umpire. It was Guus's serve and in the return I totally lost my cool and hit a really wide shot on purpose. I stood there with both my arms stretched out to the side as if I was about to direct an airplane to land and shouted loudly for everyone to hear,

*'OUT!'*

whilst looking directly at the linesman and the umpire. It obviously meant that I lost the match. If it had been a match where either of us could have progressed to the next stage I would have made an effort and fought hard for the last point. As it was, it was not going to make any difference to our ranking or results within the tournament, so I felt I needed to make a point about the linesman's ruling. Once the match was over, I shook hands with Guus so he knew I didn't hold anything against him for winning and he gave me a look which showed he understood how I felt.

Some of my team heard the shout (it really was that loud!) and turned to see what was going on. They had seen me with my arms outstretched glaring angrily at the technical officials and tried to console me when I came off the court. It was one of the rare times where I've totally lost my temper on a court and it took some time to calm me down.

At para-badminton tournaments we go out for meals in the evening together. On one occasion, we were in Spain and the restaurant was very busy. Literally as soon as one table emptied it filled up again and there were queues of people waiting to come in as we were leaving. Luckily we had an early reservation in order to be able to sit together.

There was a good group of us - around 15-20, and our order of drinks, starters and main course was a big one. Our starters all came together; I had a lovely tomato soup and the atmosphere was fun. We caught up with each other properly outside of the tournament setting. It felt like we were friends on holiday, relaxed and enjoying each other's company.

Everyone started getting their main courses but mine didn't arrive. I had ordered a simple vegetarian pizza and everyone else ordered a meat or fish-based dish. I waited and waited for it. Finally, the bill had arrived for payment and we all started working out how much each of us had to pay. We paid for the things we ate and drank only. In the middle of this, the waiter brought my pizza over. I turned to him and said

*'You will have to take it back. We have all finished and are ready to go now.'*

He looked a bit puzzled, so I repeated that everyone else had eaten and it was time for us all to leave so the pizza would have to go back and I wouldn't be paying for it. The other players offered to stay whilst I ate the pizza.

*'No. We came together, we would leave together. I will just pay for my drink and soup. I refuse to pay for the pizza that came too late to eat.'*

So they paid and left. Martin Rooke's brother-in-law spoke some Spanish so he stayed behind with me. We took the payment to the bar and asked to speak to the manager to explain about the shortfall. He came out but refused to take our explanation and went back into the kitchen bringing the chef out with him. The chef brought a big carving knife, waving it wildly in my direction. None of us wanted a fight so I said,

*'Listen, there are lots of people as witnesses. You pull a knife on me, I will call the police.'*

They didn't want the aggravation as they were incredibly busy so they agreed to let me pay just for the drink and soup and we both ran out of there very quickly, joined the others and headed back to the hotel. I was a little hungry after all the cut throat pizza excitement by the time we settled ourselves in the hotel bar. So I told the bar staff about my adventure and they rustled up a nice double decker vegetarian sandwich with salad, crisps and other small bites.

It was something that I could eat whilst we all sat in the bar with drinks and carried on socialising together. I ate a good breakfast the next day as well. Badminton burns up a lot of calories when you are playing competitively and I seriously ensure that I don't go hungry when competing to win.

## ∼ Keep Your Kit On ∼

The first time we travelled to the para-badminton tournament in Dortmund (1997) we didn't know which hotel we were staying in and had no clear instructions about the general tournament arrangements. We were simply told we'd be met at the airport so didn't think to ask about anything else at the time. When we landed we got our bags from the carousel and looked around for people carrying our names on a board at the arrivals area. We walked around the area, waited, walked around again, waited some more but no one came.

In the end we were getting a bit frustrated so I rang Jim Mackay's wife in North Wales using the public pay phones. None of us had a mobile telephone at that time. Luckily I had some small change in the local currency. She told me that the guys who were meant to meet us were there looking for us. For the next 3 hours we carried on walking around the airport. If it had been a marathon we would have been doing our lap of honour, that's how much wandering about we did. We were there for so long that players coming off airplanes from other airports around the UK recognised us and asked who they were supposed to meet and how they were to get to their hotels too!

My prosthetic side was starting to hurt by now so I was really glad when we finally decided enough was enough and it was time to take a break for refreshments. We sat at a table and were busy complaining about how bad the service and organisation was from the tournament committee because there was no one here to meet us and no news or information from anyone. It was all so inconvenient and we couldn't even go directly to the hotel because we didn't know what it was called or where it was. Just as we were in full complaining mode, a guy who was sitting at a table next to us turned and asked,

*'are you English?' 'Yes.'*

We told him that we were there to play a badminton tournament but we couldn't find the people who were supposed to pick us up. At this point he smirked with obvious relief and said,

*'That's us. We're supposed to pick you up. We've been looking all over the airport for you for the last 3 hours! We thought you'd be wearing your Badminton England team kit and would be easy to spot. That's why we didn't have your names on a board.'*

So luckily we all found each other and got on with the tournament. Now you know why people hold name cards at airports, the usefulness of mobile phones, and why, if you want to be recognised from a distance, you should keep your team kit on when travelling.

# Chapter 2
# You've Made the
# WRONG LEG!

One Saturday afternoon whilst I was still in hospital, Sister Buck took me to one side and said, 'Meva Singh, you've got some visitors in the kitchen. It's private there.'

My mind froze and my heart started thumping loudly at her words. What did she mean? Who wanted to see me and why did they want to meet me somewhere private? It couldn't be a medical issue as the staff don't usually ask to meet their patients in the kitchen, so what was going on? While my brain tried to fathom out what on earth I was letting myself in for, I wheeled myself carefully into the kitchen. There, standing straight and tall in front of me, was an imposing looking uniformed policeman. Well that really did my head in when I saw him. What have I done now? Had I been speeding? Did I have a parking ticket? In a wheelchair? Whilst I was in hospital? Was my family okay? On and on the voices went inside my head until they were interrupted by him looking at me and asking,

*'Do you want the bad news or the good news first?'*

With an uncomfortable lump in my throat I replied in a quiet shaky voice, 'Bad news first please.'

He said the bad news was that the lady who ran into me wasn't insured to drive the car. She lived in the nearby council housing estate. Her husband had just bought the car from an auction a week earlier. For some reason, she'd decided to take it out for a drive. No licence, no insurance, nothing. She wasn't concentrating on the road and simply didn't see me.

I froze numb when I heard that. No feeling. No thoughts. Nothing. Then suddenly everything inside me crumbled, like polar ice sheets breaking into the ocean. Crack! Snap! Whoo-osh. Here I was. With NO leg. My whole world turned totally upside down. And she would get away with it ALL? Scot free? No repercussions, no responsibility, no punishment, nothing. And what was I going to be left with? No job, no car, no life, a distressed family who couldn't help me see a way through this. How on earth was that even remotely fair? What sort of justice was there in this world?

She didn't even apologise for what she had done. Looking back on it now, I was so angry about everything that had happened that I probably wouldn't have accepted the apology anyway. At one point I had so much anger burning up inside me, I felt like going over to her house and beating her up; if not physically then definitely verbally. But I didn't. It took a lot of self-control to keep a lid on all the anger, hurt and pain. To not go around to her house threatening, yelling or being abusive. To not shout at her and ask her what she thought she was playing at by running me over and leaving me with no leg; even though I knew where she lived and it wasn't that far away. I was so angry I could have done that, but I didn't. It was going to take a lot of support from my family and the medical staff to help me work through the torrent of emotions that would come flooding through me at unexpected moments. Wave after gigantic wave of anger, frustration, disbelief, distress and more. Without warning. Without control. Piercing the numbness of my mind whenever I was at my weakest mentally.

As suddenly as those emotions came they went away again and I felt tired and empty inside. I slumped disheartenedly further down into my wheelchair. I'd been cheated out of a life. As a man, as a husband, as a potential father, as a son, as a brother. Really cheated. All I was now was this helpless, useless wreck. Confined to a wheelchair. Full of resentment, despairing at the futility of everything and so angry at the stupidity of the woman who had landed me in this situation. Seeing how I was battling internally with my emotions the policeman looked at me gently and said, *'I've still got some good news for you. I'm a through knee amputee myself. I lost mine whilst I was refereeing a rugby match.'*

Well my mind practically blew apart on hearing that. Now I've never played rugby. It wasn't a game we learnt in school. Badminton has always been my thing. But I have watched the game and know what the players have to do to win. Like who'd even imagine that could happen, right? If you're playing rugby then it's to be expected that you break a bone or three, lose a tooth, get a bruising or whatever. But losing your leg because you're refereeing? That must have been some game. I dread to think what happened to the players if that was what happened to the ref!

*'I'm working at Barnet police station now in the office.'*

Until that point, I'd been so worked up; simply feeling incredibly vulnerable and sorry for myself. In my wheelchair, in this small kitchen, with a tall foreboding looking police officer in front of me. That I hadn't even noticed he used a walking stick! He said he had two children and was there to encourage me and let me know that I could still do anything I want to do even though I'd lost my leg.

*'You need willpower. If you want to do it, you can.'*

His voice had a compassionate strength and positive tone to it that helped me to believe him. He asked if I had any questions about amputation and life afterwards. My thoughts went straight to my wife. It had all hit her really hard and I felt so guilty. We had barely been married for two and a half years, still living in the big family house with my mum and dad. I thought emotionally about how we first met less than 3 years ago.

I had gone to India with my mum to meet a girl and her family because I felt ready to marry and settle down. There wasn't a big enough Sikh community in England in those days and as it's a lifelong decision most of us felt we had more choice of finding suitable partners in India. It was always an exciting time in a family when someone did decide they were ready to fall in love, get married and continue the family line. The word would go out on the family and friends' grapevine; through the aunts', uncles' and neighbours' gossip channels and matchmakers would start arranging meetings. There was a particular clothing shop 'baba hati' in the town of Goraya, not far from my masar ji's (uncle's) town, Muthada Kalan which are both in the Jalandhar district of Punjab State in India; where prospective couples and families would be introduced to each other and decide whether to proceed to the stage of marriage.

It was 'make or break' and first impressions really did count at those introductions. We didn't have that much time to make a decision on this as we were only in India for about 4 weeks.

After our first week we received a message saying that a girl was interested in me so I arranged to meet her at the baba hati.

I waited and waited inside with my mum and masi ji (aunty) feeling like a total lemon when no one turned up. What a waste of time that was! It turned out that her uncle had decided that he didn't want her to go to England to live, as he found her more useful helping him at home, but I didn't know that at the time.

I felt like a complete fool hanging around there watching other couples and families meeting, chatting and knowing they probably all realised I'd been stood up. Eventually, once I'd accepted she wasn't going to show we headed back slowly to my masar ji, Gurabax Singh Aujla's house. My cousin, Baldish Kaur Aujla, noticed I was looking really down and demoralised so she asked me what had happened. When I told her she got straight into action. She told a school friend, who told her mum, who put it back out on the grapevine that there's a really handsome young guy from England looking for a bride but they'd have to be quick because we were only there for a couple of weeks.

Word eventually reached the older sister-in-law (tai ji), Satvinder Kaur Takhar, of my future mother-in-law, Sharanjit Kaur Takhar who wanted to check me out first before introducing me. Unfortunately, the day they decided to come over to my masar ji's house in Muthada Kalan we'd decided to visit relatives in the neighbouring village, Mehsampur. So we weren't even there when they arrived! No internet, no mobile phones, no landline 'phones. Nothing. No way to communicate quickly with each other if you are in the wrong place at the wrong time. So my masar ji discussed it with his wife, Chana Kaur and did the best thing he could think of. He told my cousin Baldish Kaur to jump on her bicycle, ride like a tornado over to Mehsampur and tell us to come back to his house. Which she did! And she swears to this day that she broke the women's land speed record for steel framed bicycles trying to get to me. That's how much she wanted me to meet my future wife.

When we got back to my masar ji's place we freshened up quickly. I felt so at ease with my future mother-in-law Sharanjit Kaur Takhar and her older sister-in-law Satvinder Kaur Takhar that I told them how the first girl had stood me up. They had a good laugh at that and said,

*'Ah, their loss is our gain, my son.'*

When I asked about my prospective wife I was told that they did not want us to meet at the baba hati. They wanted us to come to their village and directly meet at their house instead. So a few days later, 5 of us set off to meet my potential future wife. 3 ladies and 2 men. All excited, all dressed up. It took us two bus journeys on hot dusty roads and a bit of a walk to get to the house but I'm glad we did. I was really nervous and excited all at the same time. What if the family didn't like me? What if we didn't like any of them? What if the girl wasn't the right one?

When we arrived we had to first go and sit in the house opposite which later turned out to be my future aunty-in-law's place. There we met the grandfather Gulzar Singh Thakar, uncles and the rest of the family.

Their family are big farmers in the area and mine are small farmers so the discussions flowed nicely between us all. They decided they liked me. We agreed on the arrangements and they finally said, *'okay, you can go and meet her now.'*

This is when I met my future wife. It didn't feel real up to that point but as soon as we met and had a chance to chat I knew I'd made the right decision. Kamalpreet Kaur and I got on really well with each other. After that I met my father-in-law, Gurpal Singh Thakhar.

I am so glad that the first girl didn't turn up that day. Because, although it felt like a big disappointment initially, I really do think I got the best life partner I could ever have wished for. We have had many happy, fulfilled years of marriage together and our children and grandchildren are a true reflection of how close and loving our family unit is. It's the most important thing in my life that I am really proud of; aside from my badminton achievements. My beautiful family.

After our first meeting we went back a few days later and had the engagement ceremony. Then it was time for me to head back to England, make sure the immigration paperwork was in place and get ready for the next phase of my life as a husband, father and son-in-law. When Kamalpreet Kaur finally received the correct permit papers we were over the moon. We got married in a registry office in the middle of a cold and wet December day but waited until the fine Spring weather for the Sikh wedding. Everyone was so happy and excited, but I reckon no one was more happy and excited than the two of us. We didn't know then that just a few years later I'd lose my leg and be sitting in hospital trying to recover my sense of who I now was and deciding how I could now possibly be a good husband.

Kamalpreet Kaur lost a lot of weight over that time worrying about how things would be when I came out of hospital. She could have left me if she wanted to but she stuck by me through it all. She put up with a lot both immediately following the accident and in the many years afterwards as I came to terms with how to manage life with only one good leg when everyone else around me had two. I was used to being very active as an able-bodied person and I would always push myself hard to reach those same activity levels after I lost the leg......

I knitted my brow and bit my lip trying to control my emotions as I thought about her. The policeman interrupted my painful musings by asking me if I had any questions for him.

*'Main concern is, how am I going to have a family?'* I barked defensively as I tried to choke back the tears.

*'Don't worry about it, mate. Getting the leg over is easy. It doesn't get in the way anymore. I've got two children',* he replied, laughing kindly as he looked at my scrunched up face.

To give him credit, he had a good sense of humour for a policeman. He told me his name, Bob Green, and gave me his address in Hertfordshire. We stayed in touch for a few years afterwards until he retired. He said to come and see him at Barnet police station anytime while he was at work. He helped me come to terms with my amputation and it encouraged me to help other amputees I met throughout my life too. And he was right. My first daughter was born a year later.

Something or other always goes wrong whilst you're in hospital. It's annoying, frustrating or distressing at the time but afterwards it makes a good story! For me it was exactly the same. It didn't help that I wasn't exactly the model patient when I was in the ward so the nurses certainly had their work cut out trying to keep me disciplined and toeing the line. Especially in a ward with other patients. I mean, patients are patients, right? And ill men are always the worst they say, though as a man I stand (one-legged) to dispute that. But a couple of silly things did happen whilst I was in hospital.

Like the time I received special permission to go to the Nanak Darbar North London Gurdwara New Southgate (Sikh temple) for a few hours because my family and the Sikh community had arranged prayers after I'd lost my leg. I remember that day so well; Sunday, Aug 4th. I was only allowed out on the condition that I was NOT to drive as I was still on strong medication. Well of course I didn't listen to that bit. I simply smiled, nodded and then promptly blocked it out of my mind. It just so happened that my brother, Bakhtawar Singh, had an automatic vehicle which didn't need me to use my left leg so I asked him for the keys to drive myself to the Gurdwara. He was a bit reluctant but I assured him I was absolutely fine to drive. He knew how much I really wanted to get out of hospital and back to normal everyday life. To feel like I was a real man, a husband, a breadwinner, a badminton player. Knowing that, he eventually relented and handed the car keys over to me.

I was over the moon. The weight of those keys felt like the crown jewels burning through my hand. I hopped excitedly into the driver's seat, adjusted the mirrors and proudly set off. Steering myself out of the hospital car park in his automatic Mark III Cortina felt like breaking out of jail! Freedom. Normality. Back to being a human being! It was exhilarating even though I was just driving a short distance in heavy traffic through North London to the Gurdwara. I felt like I was in a Ferrari careering round Silverstone. I was alive! And free, so free! To live my life, go back to my family and be me again.

Well as you can imagine, absolutely everyone was so annoyed with me that day. If I've had an ear-bashing from them once about it, I've had the same lecture a hundred times since then too. Sister Buck gave me a stern look as she saw me driving off from the hospital car park and my father shouted at me angrily as I parked up confidently outside the Gurdwara.

*'You're an invalid, don't pretend you're better than you are! These people are all here to see you and you're driving?'*

To be honest I was really hurt by their reaction. I thought they'd be proud of me for facing up to driving again. After all, it was a car that knocked me down. Okay, technically I wasn't in a car myself when it happened - so I was a pedestrian but it does affect you. It does make you think:

*'What would have happened if the car I'd been driving had lost control suddenly and ploughed straight into a group of children? What if I hadn't been watching where I was driving and run over an old man crossing the road?'*

And lots of other things besides. All to do with guilt. Feeling guilty. Was it my fault that I was standing by my car at that particular time when the lady driver lost control? What if I had gone out a couple of minutes earlier or later? What would have happened then?

It certainly took some doing to explain to my family, to the medical staff and everyone else that I was getting behind the wheel of the car to drive myself to the Gurdwara because I didn't want to be scared of cars or driving after my accident. I wanted to get back behind the wheel and I wanted to show people I was ready to do it. They all calmed down eventually. But it took a while for them to forgive me and to get back on their good side again. Because of the medication I was on, that was their main concern. If I hadn't been on strong medication which had side effects that impacted on your ability to concentrate whilst operating machinery and driving then they would have been much happier about seeing me behind the wheel again.

To add to the chaos, just as everyone was thinking it couldn't get any worse, my first visit to Stanmore Limb Centre at the Orthopaedic Hospital to get my very first prosthetic limb fitted didn't go as smoothly as it could have done. The nurses woke me up on the ward at 6am. I had breakfast and got ready. It was an exciting moment. Getting fitted for my very first prosthetic leg. I couldn't wait and everyone on the ward shared my excitement with me, telling me that they hoped it would go well. The ambulance had been booked for the morning so I wasn't allowed to have lunch. Unfortunately, it didn't turn up until the afternoon to take me to Stanmore so I missed a meal. Anyone who knows me will tell you that, despite it being dreaded hospital food (wins hands down against school dinners), I am not good at going hungry. Luckily my excitement dampened the hunger pangs as soon as the ambulance dropped me off at the limb centre. The staff at Stanmore took all my measurements and then said I was free to go.

I sat in the waiting room for the ambulance to take me back from Stanmore Limb Centre to Barnet Hospital. I felt quite motivated at the thought of being able to walk again and frustrated that the prosthetic would take so long to make. They suggested the leg would be ready in around 3 weeks. It was nearly the end of August so the earliest it would be ready was the middle of September. When I thought of the last three weeks in hospital I hoped the next three would go more quickly. Perhaps they might even discharge me soon?

Staff were moving around the building as they usually do and I whiled away the time just watching the hustle and bustle around me as patients came and went. The painkillers I had been given before I left the ward were starting to wear off and it was getting uncomfortable again on my amputated side. Eventually around 5pm, one of the staff noticed I was still there and asked why I hadn't gone back to Barnet Hospital?

'No-one has come to pick me up yet,' I replied grumpily. My stomach was starting to complain that it had not had anything since breakfast and sharp pains were radiating from my stump as the painkillers lost their hold. I was not in a good mood and was starting to feel really frustrated sitting there. Just waiting. Waiting to get better enough to be discharged. Waiting for the ambulance to pick me up. Waiting until the leg was ready. Waiting, waiting and more waiting. It was aggravating and totally soul destroying.

So the receptionist had to chase around to find another ambulance that could take me back to Barnet Hospital. Apparently, although the ward nurses had booked it in both directions, the crew changed shifts at 4.30pm and the driver had forgotten to tell the next one to pick me up! I was three weeks into my hospital stay by this time and itching to get out and go home. So I wasn't at all impressed when I heard what had happened.

I had a good moan with all the patients on the ward about it when I came back and really felt that I'd had my fill of hospitals for a lifetime. A week later they finally discharged me and allowed me to go home. Total bliss! That 'get out of jail free' card was mine and I sure was going to use it.

On discharge I didn't have a wheelchair or an artificial leg, only crutches. The wheelchair I was using in hospital was for ward use only. The only other way to get a wheelchair was to hire one from the Red Cross. When I got home, social services offered to put in a toilet/bathroom downstairs and an extension to my parents' house with us paying only some of the costs of the work. But Kamalpreet Kaur and I refused because if we had done that we would have felt really bad about moving out and leaving my parents' house in that state. All those changes made to the house just because of my accident. It would be a constant reminder to my parents of what had happened and we would have had to change it all back again after we had moved out; taking up a lot of time, effort and money. Since I wasn't able to work now and didn't know what sort of work I'd be able to do once I had my prosthetic leg, we decided not to bother making those changes in the first place.

That's how I ended up hopping around on crutches everywhere for a good 4 or 5 weeks. It was a frustrating experience at times. Especially when I went outdoors. Mentally, becoming an amputee and being seen as 'an invalid' does affect you. People would shout 'peg leg' at you and other such negative things. Youngsters mainly, thinking they were being funny. That hurt. Not physically; they didn't throw anything at you like stones or punch or try to kick your crutches from you and laugh as they watched you fall over. It hurt psychologically and emotionally a lot at the time but eventually I got to the point where I didn't care what others thought. I would fight the pain and anger continuously. Phantom pains were agony and sometimes I got angry at the people closest to me. My immediate family. They really had to take the majority of the strain and difficulty of my adapting to everyday life on crutches with no left leg, even with friends that we had around us. But I kept at it because I wanted to get fit and strong again. To be as good as Bob Green, or as good as that one-legged athlete I'd seen on the television whilst in hospital. *I was not going to give up.*

In the middle of September we heard that the leg was ready for collection. My parents had no car and I was not allowed to drive yet as you have to notify the Driver and Vehicle Licensing Agency (DVLA) of your change of circumstance and apply for a modified licence. So it was a case of what now? How could I get to Stanmore Orthopaedic Hospital for the appointment? That's the time when you're glad you have good friends. And mine were friends I'd made through badminton. So I rang Mike Mansell. He was only too pleased to be able to drive me there. He dropped me off and I sat in the waiting room until it was my turn. The prosthetist came over to me and asked me for my right shoe.

*'Why do you need my right shoe?'* I asked, knotting my eyebrows in concern. *'It's the left leg that's been amputated.'*

We then discovered the limb centre had made a right leg for me and not a left leg. I went ab-solut-ely ballistic! I was boiling over with rage. I'd been struggling along for weeks without a leg and had come all that way only to find out that it wasn't ready! And not only wasn't it ready, the one they had made was THE - WRONG - LEG! Eventually they calmed me down and promised they would be able to get something ready by around 3.30pm that afternoon. It wouldn't be exactly as it should be however. They couldn't just conjure up a brand new left leg in that time. So what they were going to do was to adjust the socket they had made and put some holes in it. That way, it should fit my left stump. It was now 10.30am. I rang Mike at his office and told him the whole sorry story. He laughed sympathetically and said, *'don't worry about it, Meva, I'll pick you back up.'*

We went back to his offices in Borehamwood and I had a good moan about my first frustrating attempts at getting back on my own two feet without a leg! He helped me to get perspective on it and we both laughed together at the experience. In the afternoon, he kindly took me back to Stanmore to pick up the adjusted leg.

That very first leg was a Mappe leg. It was an all-metal leg with callipers and hinges on the side. There was a leather handle to pull so when you sat down the bottom half of the leg would collapse and allow the knee to bend. That meant you could sit on a chair with your feet flat on the floor. If that wasn't done, the knee wouldn't bend and the whole leg would stick straight out in front of you. This made for a lot of funny situations if I forgot and we had visitors to entertain! The feet were just solid round sections of wood in those days. No toes and no nails painted on them to look like the realistic feet you can get now. I didn't have a wooden foot rocker which is something that they use for very new amputees. I went straight to using wooden feet. Prosthetics have certainly come a long way since then.

**It took time and effort to get used to and accept that:**

1. **I no longer had a left leg AND**
2. **I had to work out how to use crutches properly AND**
3. **Using a prosthetic takes some doing when you haven't got a knee joint AND**
4. **Using a stick as a walking aid didn't mean I was an old man. I was still young and mostly healthy. I just had a** *slightly*, **no actually, I had a** very **different left leg.**

A lot of trial, error and understanding from your family and friends is involved whilst you go through this process. Silly things happen, frustrating things happen and funny things happen. *ALL the time.* There is never a day or week where something doesn't happen to you or your prosthetic.

For example, in November, after just a couple of months of wearing the leg, I felt confident enough to go to the local swimming pool with a friend, Alan Flashman, and his family. Alan had a farm in Totteridge which his son now runs. He and his wife Monica used to play badminton in the Flying Feathers badminton club. That's how we first became friends. So that day, I went with him, Monica and his two children, Dawn and Paul, to see if I could still swim. We reckoned there were enough of us there in case I needed any assistance.

They have a diving board in the deep end of this pool and metal steps into the shallow end. There were already children diving / jumping off the board with such obvious enjoyment by the time we got there. It was irresistible. The Mappe leg was not waterproof so I had to take it off and keep it to one side out of the way. I held the handlebars steadily and hopped one legged down the steps into the shallow end. Undeterred and not caring who else was watching, I half swam, half hopped, with noisy delight towards the middle of the pool.

At the same time, just as I was getting into deeper water to chest height, a youngster dived from the diving board. *SPLASH!* In he went in a frenzy of arms and legs curled up to create a sensation as he entered the water. His friends stood around the edge of the pool laughing at his antics. *WHOOSH,* out of nowhere, the wave of water he displaced came straight at me and knocked me over to my left side. I keeled over; it felt like I was drowning and out of control. With no left leg to keep me upright I panicked.

Seeing me struggling, Alan came in front intending to get his arms under mine to try to pull me back up. Because he came in front of me, this panicked me further. I ended up struggling and inadvertently pushing both of us underwater. Now it turns out that I am quite a strong swimmer underwater as there is no balance issue to worry about so I recovered my composure quite quickly. Unfortunately, we discovered that Alan wasn't so comfortable underwater so the lifeguard on duty ended up throwing him a ring and getting us both out of there sharpish.

The children thought this was the best adventure they'd had whilst swimming for a long time; I mean how often do you get to see grown-ups getting into trouble? Monica, Alan and I (along with the lifeguard) on the other hand all felt relieved it was over with no harm done. I'm not sure whether the lifeguard understood how much I needed to try swimming with only one leg. He didn't look too happy as we left as it probably meant he had some paperwork to fill in about the incident. Anyway, that was when I decided I wouldn't take up swimming as a sport; I would keep trying to work out how to get back into playing badminton. A sensible decision for all concerned I think.

Not long after that adventure, I went to India for three months to see my family; to show them the leg and make them feel okay about everything that had happened to me. There was so much to reassure them of, especially as we lived so far away from each other in two different countries in continents that were at least 5000 miles apart. Telecommunications for farming communities in the villages of India were still in development and air mail letters that took weeks to be delivered would not be an appropriate way to tell them about my news. The best thing to do was to get on an airplane and go over and see them all.

It was really emotional and in a way it was cathartic for me too as I'd already been through it with my immediate family. From the accident, to the recovery, to the new way I was having to live my life with a prosthetic, in a wheelchair or on crutches, I felt I had to explain it all to them calmly. Rationally. And allay their fears about the new situation in which Kamalpreet Kaur and I found ourselves. They worried a lot because they were living far away from us. They wanted to know so many things about how they could help us and whether we would be okay and able to do the normal things in life like working, having families, socialising and everything else.

I stayed in Dhesian Kahna, Jalandhar India from November to February. My family owns a farm out there so the facilities were very basic. There was no hot water system, just cold water using a hand pump so having a bath became a big event. The drainage systems were open ditches with dirty water and rubbish flowing down them and the toilets were the 'hole in the ground' style common to most rural communities at that time. In my wife's village, Sianiwal in Tehsil Nakodar, Jalandhar, they built an upright toilet that you could sit on so I was able to use it when I went to visit them.

Have you ever tried walking around on a farm with a new prosthetic leg on? It's fun but anything can happen. Like the time I was walking about on my mama ji's (uncle's) farm in the village of Mehsampur, Jalandhar. I slipped and fell as I tried to cross a drain. I heard a big snap and groaned at the thought that the leg might have broken. The hinges around the waist band just snapped and I landed with a heavy thump and plop on the soft dirty soil. Once I'd got over the initial shock and embarrassment of falling like that, I (literally) one-legged it back to the farm house. You should have seen everyone's faces full of shock and horror as I hopped in and waved my broken leg at them. What to do? What to do? They didn't want me to hop around on crutches, there was no way to get a wheelchair for the rest of the time I was there, but what to do? How on earth were they going to fix this so I could walk around everywhere again?

My mama ji, Hari Singh Maan (being the quick thinker and problem solver of the family) told everyone not to worry. He would take me to the nearby village, Begampur, Jalandhar where he knew a good blacksmith who also did some electrical welding. So off we went, huffing and puffing along at around 3 miles per hour along farm roads, going over (and sometimes down!) potholes. Me in the back of the tractor, soaking up the warm sunshine and admiring the beautiful fields and open views, my uncle driving precariously around potholes but not really managing to miss any. The tractor was an old, noisy little thing spouting out fumes, jerking and shuddering every now and again. I was half expecting it to just give up along the way and wondered what we'd do if we did get stranded out there, in the middle of nowhere. It was just open countryside for miles around with not a soul in sight to ask for help.

In my wild and fertile imagination, any number of things could have happened to us along the way. I kept a good look out for tigers, wolves, snakes and any other dangerous wildlife that I thought might be around even though I knew there wasn't. It brought back memories of my childhood when we used to play such games with my brothers and cousins. Pretending that we were being chased by wild animals and robbers and saving each other. As we wobbled and lurched from side to side along that dusty road I reflected that it was lucky that I didn't bruise easily. My years of playing badminton have made me quite tough to knocks and scrapes so the journey was a good one all in all.

When we finally got to the village and found the blacksmith, imagine our disappointment as he told us that the electricity had gone down! He could only do electrical work when it came back on again in a couple of hours. My mama ji turned round and said,

*'oh, that's fine. We're going nowhere, his leg is broken.'*

At that, the blacksmith stared at him in a sort of wide eyed, panicked confusion and growled angrily,

*'if his leg is broken then you need to take him to a doctor! I'm NOT a doctor, I'm an electrician'*

as he waved his arms around his workshop in disbelief that we couldn't see we were not in a doctor's surgery. How we both laughed when he said that. Whilst he was still looking at us in a perplexed manner wondering whether we'd been drinking or if the mid-afternoon sun had gone to our heads and made us loony, I hopped out, got the leg from the back of the tractor and showed him the broken part. At first he was shocked and then he laughed and said of course he could fix it. In fact, he did such a good job that when I got it back to Stanmore, they told me it will never break again. When I went back to visit the blacksmith in Begampur seven years later he still remembered the metal leg that he had fixed for me.

Your prosthetist is the key person in your life as an amputee. The good ones listen to you and make sure that you go home happy. I have had many different prosthetists (leg fitters) at Stanmore Limb Centre in my 40+ years as an amputee. My first prosthetist was Andrew Reid. One of my most honest leg fitters was Mark Croysdale.

He could see that I was a very active person and didn't want my prosthetic holding me back from playing badminton, working and looking after my family in London or India. So one day he said to me,

*'Meva I'm struggling with your socket mate. Do you mind if I transfer you to a lady prosthetist named Emma Gillespie who we have got at the centre? I think she can help you better than I can.'*

Mark had made me hyperbaric and suction sockets by that time but neither had worked so I knew he was genuinely concerned that he couldn't get the socket to fit as well as I needed it to. I didn't want to change prosthetists because I liked Mark but in the end I was persuaded by him and my consultant, Linda Marks, to transfer to Emma Gillespie. It turned out to be a good decision because she made my first and best sports leg for me. After she left Stanmore Limb Centre, I couldn't get a prosthetist assigned to me who was as good. This was so frustrating, so I said to my consultant Dr Sedki that I wanted to transfer to a different unit. They asked me to give them another chance and 8 years ago they introduced me to Syed who has been absolutely fantastic.

On Thursday and Friday nights after our badminton club games some of us would go to the Hand and Flowers Pub in Whetstone for a drink, a round of darts and a good catch up with the regulars. It was an old Victorian 'horse and cart style' pub where you go in one side and come out the other. As you entered there was a long old-style bar right in front of you and a dart board on the right hand side of the lounge.

Badminton would finish by around 10pm and the pubs shut at 11pm though we were allowed to hang around and finish our drinks before being kicked out at 11.15pm. The landlord knew his regulars and their drinking preferences so he'd keep your drink ready for you at the bar just as you walked in. All sorts of people used that pub. Amongst them were Post Office workers, army barracks youngsters, and older retired people living in the area. You'd see a real mix and sometimes it was so busy that we couldn't get a table so we'd just hang around the bar area with everyone else.

One winter evening, after our regular badminton club matches, I drove over to the Hand and Flowers for our usual drinks. Prosthetic legs were made of metal, so they sometimes squeak whilst you play. I parked up and decided I'd had enough of the squeaking, so I'd do something about it. There I was, car bonnet open, headlights on full so I could see what I was doing, dipstick in hand. As I stood there trying to locate the offending squeaky part of my leg, Steve Burge, a typical North Londoner strolled up beside me with some concern on his face. Steve is a good badminton player and I knew his family pretty well too. They were all local Londoners born and bred and had lived there for what seemed like forever.

*'Everything okay Meva? Whatcha doin' with your bonnet up? Something happened to the car?'*

I was concentrating so much on not losing the oil cap in the dark whilst using the dipstick that I practically jumped out of my skin and banged my head on the bonnet when he spoke. I hadn't even noticed he was there! When I'd recovered (luckily, I was wearing my turban so it didn't hurt that much) I showed him what I was doing.

*'Just oiling my leg to stop it squeaking like an irritating mouse before I go in.'*

When he heard that he burst out laughing in relief and sauntered into the pub to tell everyone.

*'ere, he's got his pants down outside, he's just oiled his leg'*

In my defence I did have shorts underneath my tracksuit bottoms, which is what he meant by 'pants.' It made everyone laugh and from then on, I was teased about it on a regular basis every time I came to the badminton club.

*'ere Meva, oiled her up yet? D'ye need any lubricant on that?'*

It's all WD40 nowadays so no need for car engine oil but it certainly came in handy when I needed it.

Whetstone had a very busy shopping area and is otherwise known for being the location of the Soviet Spy news agency TASS. They had a radio monitoring station in Whetstone, for which Churchill had given permission in 1941, in order for the Russians to gather news to broadcast back to their citizens (it has to be remembered that Russia was on the side of the allies during the Second World War). There were 6 Pubs in High Road Whetstone in those days, (1980's). The Griffin, Blue Anchor, Black Bull, Three Horseshoes, Bull and Bush and our local, The Hand and Flowers. And we also used to go to The Orange Tree Pub in Totteridge every now and again which is still very popular. The Griffin and The Three Horseshoes are the only ones that are still operating as pubs in Whetstone.

The Hand and Flowers was demolished around 1985 and is now a Barclays bank. The landlord, a retired army sergeant and his wife, Ken and Bettie Bellinger Smith, lived upstairs and it always had a homely, comfortable feel to it. They had been there since 1972. Ken and Bettie even had individual old style drinking tankards made for the regulars to use with their names on them. After they sold The Hand and Flowers, they moved on to another pub called the York Arms in 1984 which they ran with their family until it closed down in 2020 during the height of the Covid-19 pandemic.

## ⚬ When a Clutch Gets You Disqualified! ⚬

I always play to win. I don't think it's worth playing if you're not going to win. That was how strong I was mentally about my ability after I lost my leg. Partly that had to do with wanting to inspire other amputees to reach for higher things as well as to show that I was tough, the best there was and no pushover. Winning something made me feel really good about myself and each time I played in the British Amputee

Sports Tournament Weekends at Stoke Mandeville in Aylesbury, I would always come away with singles and doubles medals. It's all in the mindset and this had been drilled into me by everyone I'd played with over the years in the badminton clubs. At the amputee tournaments I would try to get that same message over to other amputees. That joining a badminton club could help them achieve a lot in their lives too.

With every track record of achievement there is always a 'one time it didn't happen' story. That became true for me too in my 8th year as an amputee. I was actually disqualified from playing in a tournament because I was late for the match. Well you can just imagine it can't you? Was I fuming? You bet I was!

*'15 minutes that's all. You could have switched the rota to play other players first'* I shouted at them angrily.

But it didn't make any difference. They just turned around and said that I should let someone else win for a change. It really made my blood boil. I thought they would at least have given me and my doubles partner a second chance. (We never played with the same doubles partner in the amputee tournaments. We had names pulled out of a hat so we could all get to know each other a bit.)

Disqualified! All because of my car breaking down in Barnet! It's the only time I've been angry with Mitsubishi cars. Usually they are so reliable but on the one day when it mattered the car let me down. I'd been excited about going to Stoke Mandeville to meet up with some of the amputee regulars and to support newer amputees coming along, when the clutch went as I was driving. The only adaptation I had on the car was to put hand controls in. It was a manual car, not an automatic so I still needed to use the clutch to change gears. As I got out of the car I felt like kicking it, swearing at it, hopping up and down angrily and generally showing how mad I felt because it had broken down.

I couldn't ring ahead and let the tournament organisers know what had happened. The roads to Stoke Mandeville were all quiet country lanes not motorways so there were no public 'phone boxes around. Nothing else for it but to stand there panicking, getting stressed out and frantically looking for someone to flag down. .

The guy I eventually flagged down asked me what was going on. I told him I needed a lift to Barnet or Totteridge and he said he was going to Totteridge to play golf at the White Hart Golf Club. He understood the gist of the story and the predicament I was in, told me to just leave the car where it was and dropped me home. On the way I told him I only had one leg and he was shocked because he hadn't even noticed. I was really grateful to have been assisted by such a Good Samaritan. A total stranger who was happy to go out of his way to make sure I got home safely.

Now you'd think at this stage I'd decide not to bother going to Stoke Mandeville and just let everyone else get on with it wouldn't you? Not me. Not when there's a chance of winning another badminton final at stake! I wanted to see my name on that doubles trophy and no broken-down car was going to get in my way. So what did I do as I got to the door? I did what any self-respecting competitive badminton player would do. I dashed into the house, grabbed my wife's car keys off the side table, shouted something about taking her car and before she'd got a chance to even comprehend what was going on I (one) legged it out the door and sped off down the road driving as fast as was legally possible.

In 7 years I hadn't lost one doubles game and that disqualification in year 8 really hit me and my reputation as a player. Not only did it affect me, it meant that my doubles partner was disqualified too and he hadn't done anything to deserve that. He saw how upset and angry I was after the effort I'd made to get over there. He dealt with his own disappointment in true badminton style by beating me in the singles matches so he came away with one medal at least whilst I got nothing. Yep, that really cheered me up no end don't you think?

All in all it was a bit of a disastrous episode in my amputee badminton history. Because of a faulty clutch on a Mitsubishi. Luckily for me it happened on a weekend when Kamalpreet Kaur didn't need her car otherwise I'd have really been in for a hard time. Anyone who's married will tell you that if you ever upset your wife or do something she doesn't like then you're in for quite an ordeal until she forgives you. And Kamalpreet Kaur was no different. The car was still where I'd left it when I got back to London and we rang the AA who towed it over to the nearby garage to get it fixed. It took me quite a while to forgive Mitsubishi for that broken clutch but I have stayed a loyal customer of theirs ever since.

I've only ever won the full court singles once at those amputee national tournaments. I got into the finals at least 6 times but usually lost against below knee amputee players at that stage. I've still got the singles trophy. It's called the John Watterson Trophy. The very first amputee to win it was DC Ferne of Richmond in 1965 which was the first year the Amputee Games actually started. They were all playing full court singles matches with the old rules of scoring at that time. Nowadays we play half court singles with the new rules of point scoring. I was the very last person to win the John Watterson Trophy in 1990. The Amputee Games' weekends stopped being organised after that as the amputee associations went through a process of amalgamation.

Richard Coates of Gloucester won the John Watterson Trophy 5 times. I remember I played my first game against him. He had two hands missing. He worked in a paper mill and one day a guillotine came down and chopped off both his hands. So, he had a hook on his left arm for the shuttle and his racquet was screwed onto his right arm. He was around 10 years older than I was; a really good player but he didn't have much competition before I came along. For 3 consecutive years we would meet in the final and he would keep beating me. He moved well, was very tall, 6ft plus, and had greater fitness than me because he had both his legs. I always tried my best against him though and took him to 3 games with close scores in each. He left badminton and switched to golf in the end. Whichever sport he participated in he would always play to win.

## ∼ Wheelchair Player Did a Forecourt Runner ∼

Following a full day's play in a tournament in Ireland we had a meal to celebrate one of the para-badminton player's 40th birthday. There were around 20 people in the restaurant from areas all around the 4 Nations. Just as we had got settled with drinks and orders a uniformed policewoman approached our table. At first glance we thought it was part of the birthday joke, that someone had hired a stripogram for the birthday boy.

The next thing we saw was a male uniformed policeman come in and ask specifically for one of our wheelchair players. That shocked us into the realisation it wasn't a joke at all, but we couldn't understand what it was all about. The policeman asked him to 'step outside with his carer so they could have a chat' which he did. We continued to celebrate the birthday party hoping it was nothing too serious.

As we were tucking into our main course, our team-mate rolled back into the restaurant with his carer looking perplexed and a bit sheepish. We asked him what it had been about. He wouldn't tell us initially so none of us pressed him as it was obvious that he was feeling uncomfortable. Eventually we got to the bottom of it and it's something that a lot of wheelchair users will be able to relate to. The wheelchair player and his carer had driven to Ireland via the ferry from Liverpool and obviously had to stop for petrol along the way to Dublin.

When you drive into a petrol station forecourt after a long journey what normally happens is that the wheelchair user starts to fill up the petrol tank and the carer goes in to pay the bill. Sometimes they also go in to use the toilet and buy some drinks, snacks etc. for the rest of the journey. So that is exactly what our wheelchair team-mate thought had happened. He filled up the tank and got back in the car as he did not need to use the toilet, his carer went into the kiosk and came back out and they drove off. Little did our wheelchair friend realise that the carer had paid for snacks/drinks and gone to the toilet but had forgotten about the petrol.

That was 2 days ago. We all had English number plates and the petrol station forecourt had cameras which recorded the cars on the forecourt. The police had been called in to locate the owner of the vehicle and sort the matter out. It turned out that our wheelchair badminton friend and his carer had to return to the petrol station with the police following close behind them, pay the overlooked bill and then come back to the restaurant. That was why it took them over 20 minutes to get back to the party with us. He was reluctant to tell us about it because it was all very embarrassing. It had been a bit of a misunderstanding and miscommunication between the wheelchair player and his carer but it was all sorted out now he said. Once everyone got over the shock and embarrassment of it we all had a good laugh and it's something that we tease him about every now and again too. He felt a lot better once he had told us about it and we were relieved to know it all ended well.

## ∾ Shower Seat Paid Hotel Bill! ∾

I was sharing a hotel room with Martin Rooke during a tournament in Ireland. We had flown from Luton airport together and hired a car in Dublin. I was the driver for that tournament. We had finished our first day and I felt in need of a good shower. Badminton is a strenuous sport and I wanted to get rid of the sweat as soon as I could, especially around the stump of my left leg. It's something that is drilled into amputees continuously. No matter how active we are, amputees need to look after the skin of their stump to minimise the risk of infection, ulceration or wounds. Such issues reduce the ability to wear a prosthetic for long periods of time throughout the day leaving them reliant either on crutches or a wheelchair. In my case that would do my badminton game no good whatsoever.

The force of the hot water hitting my tired skin felt good and I languished on the shower seat enjoying the steam and heat and the clean feeling as long as I could, knowing I would have to vacate the bathroom soon enough so that Martin could get showered too. My muscles didn't ache so much now, and I was invigorated and happy. It was a good place, and I was enjoying the tournament. When I had finished, I switched off the shower, grabbed my towel and dried myself off. I held onto the handlebar attached to the wall to lift myself up off the shower seat.

CRACK!

The handlebar broke off and I fell forwards, bumping my head. Luckily not too seriously. There was a scratch and some bleeding but no concussion, broken bones, or anything like that. Once I had recovered and got changed, I rang down to reception and told them what had happened. They made a note of it and asked that we fill out a proper report in the morning before going to the tournament so they could arrange to get it fixed. We did that and carried on enjoying ourselves playing badminton. It didn't get fixed whilst we were there, so I had to be extra careful when showering for the next couple of days.

On check out the manager was on duty and said that we could both have the room stay for free because they had been unable to get the handlebar fixed. It was a bigger gesture than we expected but he explained that as we weren't going to make an accident claim against the hotel it was the least he could do.

From that day on, Martin Rooke said he would always share a room with me at badminton tournaments because it means he gets a free weekend stay

## ∼ Wheelie Tears Skirt Off! ∼

I used to enjoy the Amputee Games weekends at Stoke Mandeville in Aylesbury (late 1980's). Amputees would come from all over the UK to compete and catch up with each other as it usually only took place once a year. We would stay in the dormitory at Stoke Mandeville and eat in the canteen together in the sports building. On the Saturday night they used to have a disco with a bar. The event was mostly for amputees and their carers / family members so people would either be in wheelchairs, using crutches or on prosthetics. That particular night the dance floor was packed and there were only 3 wheelchair users at the event.

While we were all dancing, I saw one of the wheelchair users head to the dance floor with her friends. I recognised her from playing badminton earlier in the day. She played badminton standing up but had to use a wheelchair in the evening to allow her stumps to heal over again. She was really good on the dance floor doing wheelies, turns and spins so easily. It looked impressive. I turned to her when she had finished and said as a joke, *'hey that looked cool. Bet I can do that too!'*

Laughing she replied, *'come on then, dance floor is emptier now, let's give it a try.'*

She had her prosthetics on so she got out of the wheelchair and I sat in it. She showed me how to wheel it back and forth and how to hold the wheels with both hands and shift my body weight to get the front footplate and caster wheels off the ground. A wheelie is quite a difficult thing to do if you are not a regular wheelchair user. You must really engage your stomach muscles and it takes a good dose of confidence to stay in position and do the more expert turns and 360 degree spins she was doing on the dance floor.

It was a challenge and as she was standing behind me most of the time to help me balance, I felt I could master it. So, she came around to the front of the wheelchair and suggested I try it on my own. It was an exciting moment. I was in the mood to show off and prove I could do it even though that was probably the first time I'd used a wheelchair since leaving hospital more than 5 or 6 years previously. I blame it all on the alcohol in the atmosphere. I wasn't drunk as I didn't drink alcohol, but I was fairly high on enthusiasm that evening. I had played some good matches, had lots of useful conversations with the regular amputee crowd and helped to settle the newcomers into the event. Literally, I was on a roll that weekend and doing a wheelie would just top it off nicely I thought.

The DJ started playing a punchy energetic number and I decided to give it my best shot. I rolled back, pushed my weight into the chair and was about to push quickly forward but totally mistimed it and ended up rocking too far backwards.

BANG!

Down I went in the chair, landing awkwardly on my back and side with my turban rolling off my head. On the way down I reached for the nearest thing I could grab to stop myself from falling as instinct always tells you to do. Unfortunately for me this just happened to be the girl's skirt which tore away from her as I went down! It turned out that the wheelchair she uses didn't have anti-tip stoppers on the back, but I didn't know that small, vital, safety fact at the time. Luckily for everyone I wasn't hurt, the only thing that took a serious bruising was my ego (and, maybe, her modesty!). It made a good story for the other amputees who were there that weekend. They thought the whole incident was hilarious. We all laughed a lot together every time one of us remembered that night.

The Amputee Games weekends eventually came to a stop when the organisations went through a process of re-structuring. In 2009 an amputee run charity known as LimbPower was launched to organise 'Introduction to Sports' weekends for children and adults with limb deficiencies. LimbPower became a national disability sports charity in 2014 and badminton remains one of the key elements of those weekends. I have helped at most of these weekends over the last 10 years, either coaching badminton or fundraising for the charity.

It was during one of these weekends that I came across Bahman Abadani, a quadruple amputee since February 2011. He has had to overcome many hurdles during the last 10 years which have been challenging both physically and mentally. Bahman had always enjoyed sports but found that becoming a quadruple amputee made it difficult to find a sport that would match his ability. Nine months after his amputation, he attended a LimbPower Games weekend at Stoke Mandeville. He met up with a lot of amputees that weekend, tried out the sports on offer and then wandered over to where I was showing amputees how they could play badminton.

Playing badminton without one hand or one leg is challenging enough but to be without both hands and legs was initially a mind-blowing proposition for me as a coach that day. We worked out that he would need a sports arm with the racquet screwed on to it. I recommended that he approach his limb centre to see if they could help. Bahman took the suggestion to the limb centre and then to Martin, an engineer in a charity known as Remap. Martin designed and made a racquet to fit Bahman's prosthetic hand which has enabled Bahman to play badminton on a weekly basis and we have become good friends.

# Chapter 3
# Dhesian Kahna, Punjab to London, England: Family Matters

My family first came to London from the Punjab, India in 1968 when I was 13 years old; the same year that Enoch Powell's 'rivers of blood' speech was broadcast. We all lived together in a place known as Southall, 4 families under one roof, in my uncle's house. That was a time when people cared for each other. I was the oldest child in my dad's family; I've got one brother and two sisters younger than me.

At that time, Southall was experiencing a large-scale wave of immigration, but it certainly wasn't the first. The growth and change in population and infrastructure in Southall (housing, transport, schools, shops and leisure facilities) have been well documented right back to 830 AD. Throughout the years of the two world wars in the 20th Century, Belgians, Germans, Polish, Austrian and Jewish people came to the area; either fleeing persecution as refugees or because of their fighting roles within the war effort. In the 1920s/30s a lot of Welsh people came in search of a way out of poverty because the increasing industrialisation and urbanisation in London provided more jobs than the rural landscapes of Wales.

Literally there was so much work going on with the expansion of Heathrow airport, flour mills, rubber and chemical factories (Quaker Oats, Woolfs Rubber) and all the rebuilding effort after the war years that people just kept coming. In search of work, in search of a better life. The labour shortages were partly caused by local people deciding that the jobs on offer were not 'good enough' for them to do. They were either too dirty, too difficult, or did not pay as much as they would expect. So, factory owners did the next best thing they could think of which was to source labour from Commonwealth countries such as India and the Islands of the Caribbean.

That was how between 1945-48 the Windrush Generation became just one of many Commonwealth immigrant populations that found themselves settling in and around the Southall area. Families from South India, Pakistan, Bangladesh and Ugandan Asians expelled by Idi Amin soon added to the rich cultural mix. It was estimated that during the late 1980's at least 65% of the population of Southall was made up of people from the Asian subcontinent. Nowadays there are also Somali families and those from many European nations all living side by side in this vibrant multicultural area of London.

As children we didn't realise that our families coming to Southall with a view to staying for a lifetime in the area would cause some of the longer-term local residents to take major offence at our need for things from our home countries; our food, language, religion and community activities. For us it was all so exciting that we could go and watch a Bollywood film at the Dominion Cinema with our cousins or tune into the latest bhangra hits on Sunrise Radio even though we were in a very English country. It felt like we were accepted as part of the community and London was our home. The people, sights and sounds of Southall were the beginning and end of our whole world.

For some people, the fact that so many non-white children were in one school really upset them. Between 1965 and 1975 London councils decided that children of immigrants should be bussed to different schools further away in neighbouring council areas to help them to become more used to speaking English as their first language. For the local inhabitants in those neighbourhoods though it really was all about the colour of our skins and our different ways / mannerisms. We were referred to as 'people of colour' 'black' 'nigger' 'paki' and lots of other negative, offensive, derogatory, and insulting terms. It was as if people felt they had the right to look down on us because we were new to the country and looked different to them

Southall experienced a lot of negative publicity during the 1970's, just a few years after I arrived in the country. There was the fascist skinhead march in 1970, the murder of Gurdip Singh Chaggar in 1976 and, the most brutal of all, the killing of schoolteacher Blair Peach on St George's Day, 1979 at an anti-fascist demonstration against the National Front. Even Clarence Baker, of the band Misty in Roots, spent

5 months in a coma following a violent attack! That day, the police were at their worst. Batons, truncheons, blood and tears filled the news for days afterwards. It was as if the National Front and the police were making sure that Enoch Powell's dreadful words uttered in 1968 would come true. The words of an extreme right-wing politician who did not want people of any other colour except white in the country, did not agree with inter-racial marriage and would speak of 'pure blood lines' in a similar tone to those of the Nazis.

Movements such as the National Front, British National Party and other far right extreme white supremacy groups retained followers right through into the 21st century even though their more violent views and actions were kept under tighter control by the general population. People just became more civil to each other once they finally accepted that we were all here to stay and we just got on with life. Unfortunately, even though we are now in the third decade of the 2000's, the words of hate and division are just as loud and disgraceful now as they were then. History really is trying very hard to repeat itself using different external world events as excuses to create difficulties for communities who work hard to make a place their home. No doubt coronavirus and its numerous variants will engender yet another excuse.

Obviously when we first arrived, we couldn't all stay in a small semi-detached house for the long term as we were growing children and needed space to study and play. So for a short time I stayed with my grandfather, (or Nana ji as we called him), Gurbachan Singh Maan. He owned a restaurant called The Punjab which has been in Neal Street, Covent Garden, London WC2 since 1951. It first opened in 1946 before moving to Neal Street and it's still run by the fourth generation of my mum's side of the family in 2021. Tourists and theatre visitors from all over the UK and the world come to taste the exquisite curries, naan breads, chutneys and other Punjabi traditional foods that are listed on the menu.

My mama ji (mum's brother), Darshan Singh Maan, also owned two restaurants in London. One called New Punjab, in Goodge St, Fitzrovia W1 which he owned fully and the other called Sardar in Tottenham Court Road, W1 which he owned in partnership with his son-in-law Balbir Singh Bains and nephew Sital Singh Maan. He had been a serving member of the British Army and had arrived in the UK in 1948. He lived in Finchley, so we already knew a little bit about the area before we moved there.

I remember spending at least two weeks in Central London at my Nana ji's place; the best time of my life because I spent a lot of it with him. The thing I most remember was going to Trafalgar Square to feed the pigeons together. We would always buy bird food from the same guy from the same hut. For sixpence, the old sixpence (a tanner), which would be worth 2 ½ pence if the half pence piece was still in circulation..

From there our family moved to Seven Kings and lived in rented accommodation near my second mama ji (uncle), Pritam Singh Maan. I went to the same school as my cousin, Satnam Singh Maan who is now the owner of Major Builders Merchants based in Ilford, Essex. At this school, I was surprised because we would all get free milk to drink at 10.15 every morning. I joked with the schoolteachers and classmates how amazing it was that we didn't have to feed the cows and buffalos to get milk. It came directly from a bottle / container. And we didn't have to pay for it either. The school was giving it to us for free. They don't give free milk in schools nowadays, in the 2020's, but the need for free school dinners is very much a hot topic for low-income families with celebrity footballers such as Marcus Rashford supporting such campaigns.

School summer holidays were spent in Central London at my Nana ji's restaurant with my third mama ji, Piara Singh Maan, my mami ji (aunt) Amar Kaur, and their three children, (my cousins) Pal Kaur, Satnam Kaur and Mohan Singh. The restaurant was really busy between 12pm-3pm so the adults didn't want us running around and getting in their way whilst trying to serve customers. At that time there were only 2 channels available on a black and white television, which was boring, so Mohan Singh, Satnam Kaur and I, being inquisitive teenagers, used to go to Trafalgar Square, Covent Garden Fruit and Vegetable Wholesaler's Market when it was in Needle Street, (before it moved to Nine Elms in November 1974) and Regent's or Hyde Park.

We had plenty of time to kill so we just went out and explored. Discovering everything in the city was a new, exciting experience for me; Seven Dials, Drury Lane, Oxford Street, Leicester Square, Soho, the nightclubs. We used to pass Stringfellows all the time and not know how famous a place it was. I saw more of Central London then than I've ever seen since. All so different from my home in Dhesian Kahna, India. But no matter where we went, we'd always come back around 2.45pm so we could eat a good lunch after all the customers had gone. No way was I going to miss out on the delicious prawn bhuna which was my favourite dish when I was younger.

One Friday lunchtime, when I was of school leaving age, I went to Nana ji's restaurant to visit. He had sold the business to my cousin Sital Singh Maan by that time as he was getting too old to continue with the long hours and strenuous work. My other cousin Resham Singh Maan closed the restaurant after the lunchtime rush and took his wife to the doctor's surgery for a check-up. They said they would be back before opening time which was 5.30pm so I sat and chatted with Nana ji. Time was going by and they still hadn't returned.

*'Ki karenga, Nana ji? (What should we do?)*

I asked, pointing my head towards the door where customers had started to queue. He told me to let them in. The first customer was a regular who knew exactly which table he was going to sit at and didn't need a menu because he always ordered the same thing - 1 pint of lager and 4 poppadums with onion chutney.

My older cousins came in to help. I stayed until 8.30pm. I enjoyed working there so I started off helping out in the school holidays and then worked full time Sunday to Friday, helping out the Lester's in their greengrocer's shop on Saturday when I left school for one year. Sital Singh Maan's son, Amritpal Singh Maan is now a managing director of Punjab Restaurant. He was named in the 2022 New Year's Honours List for an OBE award for his services to charity and community. He sponsored nearly £1 million worth of meals and provided over 200,000 meals to those in need since the Covid pandemic began in the UK in March 2020 alongside other philanthropic and community activities. The whole family are so proud of him.

I left to work full-time for Derek Lester after that year because it was closer to where I lived in Finchley Central. The pay and hours they were offering (Mon-Sat 7am-6pm, with a half day off on Thursday) suited me better as it meant I could go back to enjoying playing badminton.

I came to the UK from India so long ago now that I feel as though I've lived in Finchley Central all my life. My father, Ajit Singh Dhesi, first started working in a factory making concrete slabs in Hayes. After moving to Finchley Central, he worked in a bakery and then in an engineering factory making tools for lathes. In those days it was easier to find a job and people often left one place of work on Friday and started a new job on Monday without too much difficulty.

My mum Amar Kaur worked in Finchley Central for the soft drinks firm, Corona. She used to check that every bottle was labelled and refill the labelling machine. Others would check that bottles were filled. If any were missed, they were taken out, refilled and relabeled, and put back on the conveyor belt. There was never a suggestion that any of us wouldn't find work whilst living in London. Having a good Sikh community nearby and an extended family working in the restaurant business made us all want to work hard and succeed too.

I was never any good at education. In India my family (on both my dad and my mum's side) were mainly farmers. I went to the same village school in Dhesian Kahna as my father did when he was young. His dad's brother (chacha ji) was the teacher there. By the time I got there, his chacha ji had retired from teaching. The school only went up to year 5 (juniors) because there weren't enough children in the village to keep it going for the older ones. I had to go to the neighbouring village school in Bundala for one year and back to Dhesian Kahna school the following year. It had expanded to year 8 pupils and the head of the village, Sarpanch Mahinder Singh, who I used to call baba ji, asked us to come back to finish our studies there. It didn't take long to walk to school as it was less than half a mile away but obviously we were walking in bright, hot, sunshine most of the time. Unlike in London where we didn't know if it was going to be wet, foggy, snowing or windy until we woke up in the morning and looked out the window.

In the UK, (apart from the short time I went to school with my cousin) I spent the most time at Alder Boys' School in East Finchley, which was nearly a mile away from our house. If you wanted to catch the bus it was a penny each way, two bus changes and you still had to walk a long way to the main entrance. So we shelved the 'going by bus' idea and just walked there instead, no matter what the weather was like. When I first started it took a while to make friends with other boys because I couldn't understand the language. I couldn't speak any English, only Punjabi, but I soon became friends with a boy who was also good at math and we both competed with each other to get top marks. The teacher would give our class the challenge that if you got 10 sums done then you could go to the front of the queue for assembly and not have to line up with everyone else. So that's what we did and it's probably where I discovered my passion for wanting to come first and win at everything (okay, basically, I realised I just didn't like queuing).

We had 4 schoolhouses: Archers (Red), Foresters (Green) Rovers (Blue) and Rangers (yellow). Black uniform, an alder tree green badge and a green striped tie. I was in the Archers House. We all used to compete for our houses and the top house won a trophy. The boys who won the most points for their house received certificates. Our headmaster, Mr Heard, a tall, good-looking man, was very strict. We always had to have our shoes polished and our hair no longer than our ears. If it was longer, he'd tell us to get our hair cut. In 6th form we didn't have to wear uniforms so most of us wore smart casual clothes, never jeans or trainers in school. It was nothing like Grange Hill or Waterloo Road or like any of the American teenage school television programmes that are on Amazon, Disney, Netflix, HBO or Hulu.

Alder School in East Finchley was a boys' school when I went there from 1968 to 1973; a yellow brick building with an interesting history. It started out being known as East Finchley Board School or Long Lane School which taught boys, girls and infants from the mid-1880s. It was renamed Alder Council School in 1931. There were two separate entrances which were used for boys and girls when it became a mixed secondary school. In 1956 it changed again to become an all-boys' school. It closed in 1978 and the building was later demolished. When they say that education is a tough industry to be in, I guess I believe them just looking at my school alone over the years.

We had some very high-profile teachers before I got there too. Jeff Nuttall and Bob Cobbing taught at Alder School in the 1960s. They were famous for their fantastic work with art, film, music, poetry and publishing. I preferred to do practical things such as woodwork. At 16yrs of age, we had to do a set of exams known as O levels or CSE's. They are called GCSE's now, I think. I got Grade 1 in my woodwork exams, and I was good at maths. The woodwork teacher Mr Hammon was my favourite. He always had a lot of time for me.

The only other O level I got was art. The art teacher Miss Lambert got really annoyed at me because I wasn't making any effort. She said,

*'if you don't hand the work in we can't mark it,'*

so her scolding was the inspiration that made me sit down and do it. I did 10 charcoal drawings in the kitchen all in one night. There was charcoal everywhere! When my mother came in to make some tea for breakfast in the morning all she could see was a little black boy bent over at the kitchen table and wondered where her son had disappeared to!

Before she became Prime Minister, Margaret Thatcher was a Member of Parliament for Finchley. She was supposed to visit us at the school as part of her role as Education Secretary. I had made a fruit bowl especially to give her that day. Unknown to all of us children, the Prime Minister of the day, Ted Heath had issued a three-line whip where all MPs had to go into Parliament.

Knowing the children would be disappointed, the school headmaster resourcefully got someone who looked like her to do an impersonation at the event instead. We certainly didn't know the difference that day!

To date there have only ever been two women Prime Ministers in the UK. They were both Conservative Party leaders: Margaret Thatcher (1979-1990) and Theresa May (2016-2019). They both had very difficult jobs to do whilst they were in power. Margaret Thatcher had to deal with high levels of unemployment and discontent amongst workers, unions and miners as well as trying to create closer ties to the European Union, all in addition to leading the UK during the Falklands War. Theresa May had to deal with the aftermath of a disaffected population that no longer wanted to be part of the European Union and wanted her to take them out via Brexit.

When I was older and had left school, Margaret Thatcher came door to door canvassing to our street. She would see if there were any elderly who couldn't get to the polling station and take them in a vehicle so they could vote. Margaret Thatcher was a greengrocer's daughter and I had worked in a greengrocers at the weekends whilst at school, so I felt I had something in common with her. She knocked on my door and I rudely told her (as most do!) that I was Labour. To my surprise, she said to listen to what she had to say, which I did, and she converted me to Tory (Conservative) that day! I've been Tory ever since.

I moved to East Barnet and Totteridge when I started working and raising a family. There are a lot of famous successful people connected with Totteridge and Finchley such as George Michael, David Jason, Spike Milligan, Elaine Page and Arsene Wenger. So I felt I was in a place where people made it and made it big.

I was born into a Sikh family, but I didn't follow the religion in any dedicated way whilst I was growing up. It's only since I lost my leg and I felt that God saved my life that day that I turned to my faith to give something back. I now wear a turban; I've grown a beard and I'm 100% vegetarian. I also don't drink alcohol or smoke and, although it has taken a lot of willpower, I am learning and getting stronger about it every day. The term 'Sikh' means learning. Sikhs are fighters, determined and friendly, but they will step in if someone is doing something wrong. A motto that I use regularly is 'Hit me once and I'll hit you back twice.' It has served me well to ensure that my family and I are well respected within our community and within the sport of badminton.

In fact, I am well known for my trendy turbans within the badminton community. I've worn lots of different colour turbans and even had a white turban with a red band on it to match the England kit. With the turban and the metal leg there was no way anyone could miss noticing me on the badminton court. If it intimidated my opponent a little bit, then it could only increase my chances of winning, which I was always determined to do. I now wear a bandana rather than a full turban whilst playing. It is cooler and I keep my long beard tied up during a match but prefer to open it up afterwards or whilst at home.

I go to the Nanak Darbar North London Gurdwara (Sikh Temple) in New Southgate. The good thing about London is that whatever religion you are, there is a place where you can go to practice your faith. There are temples, churches, synagogues, mosques, and many other places where you can simply go and feel spiritually connected with the world around you. Where you can restore your inner peace, and where you are accepted and supported, especially when you are trying to deal with the tragic and traumatic situations that sometimes take place within highly populated cities.

Whenever I've needed help and sponsorship, I've found most of the communities more than willing to contribute if I ask them. Whether they are Sikh, Jewish, local Londoners or friends, family and neighbours. The Sikh community from all areas of London (North, South, East and West) and the Totteridge local community always help me raise money for charities such as LimbPower which help amputee youngsters and adults to get into sports.

## ∼ Something Smells Fishy ∼

It all started when Dr Jim Mackay telephoned me on New Year's Day 1994. I'd had another operation on my leg in July 1992 so he surprised me by asking,

*'How about being part of the team going to Holland (The Netherlands), Meva? Interested?'*

Was I interested? Was he joking? Of course, I was interested! I was more than interested. It was a big honour to be asked. Once I'd got over the initial shock and excitement of the telephone call, I realised I only had around 3 months to get fit enough to compete. I was so glad he rang that day. It changed my outlook on life 100%.

Before that telephone call I had been seriously thinking of giving up badminton for good; the operation had not been as successful as initially hoped. I had been sitting in my living room looking at all the medals I had won over the years in the Amputee Games weekends organised by the British Amputee Sports Association. There was no longer any challenge in it as there had been in the competition weekends when I first became an amputee.

I was winning my matches too easily, so it wasn't as much fun as playing against a tougher competitor.

All in all, before Jim rang, I was feeling low, miserable and incredibly sorry for myself; lost in morose thought, deep in a negative spiral of hopelessness. Then Jim Mackay, with one short telephone call, gave me the best New Year's Day Resolution anyone could ever wish for; the impetus to focus on solid recovery after my leg operation and the challenge to regain my fitness to compete. To win! To go out to The Netherlands and to play my best game to win! From that New Year's Day in 1994 I have never looked back. A whole new challenging world of opportunity and friendships had been opened up for me that made any problems and issues I faced with my leg just melt away into insignificance.

I went to The Netherlands with my brand new sports leg, the IP Smart which I'd had for around 18 months. The socket was black carbon fibre with a nice semi-computerised knee that gave swing phase feedback. Sports legs always have the best knees, and changing knees from normal daily use to sports use makes life frustrating. The Netherlands was one of my earliest tournaments as an amputee. Blatchford prosthetic manufacturers sponsored this leg. I had 3 legs at that time. The battery that powered the semi-computerised knee would last 2-3 months so I was given two batteries each time. The leg had a waist band as well to keep it in place, so it felt safer to use for high impact, quick movement. There were no shoulder straps.

The Dutch tournament was the first one where they saw disabled people playing standing up or in wheelchairs. It was the very first para-badminton international ever to be held with only two countries taking part. The Netherlands and England. Their players sat down on the floor and played whilst our players used wheelchairs, stood or sat in order to play. After seeing us playing they got rid of the sitting down on the floor category as it didn't provide the same level of excitement within the game as standing or using a wheelchair. It was too static; impossible to reach the back of the court as easily sitting down, and players complained of neck and back pain when playing from a seated position.

On the day we were travelling to the Netherlands, the minibus came from North Wales with Dr Jim Mackay, his girlfriend, and a player from up north. Players went with their own cars to the meeting point to meet the minibus. Luckily there were no hold ups or delays on the roads and the minibus got to us on time. The fun and adventure all started when we got to the ferry port and tried to check in. We were told our ferry was stuck in France and wouldn't be coming. It was cancelled.

What on earth? There we were, due to compete in our first ever international tournament, stuck on the wrong side of the Channel. We were offered passage on a commercial cargo vessel instead which was travelling from Harwich to the Hook of Holland and, as we had no option, we decided to take it. It was a P&O cargo vessel that went back and forth across the North Sea and was used to transporting trucks rather than people.

Dr Jim Mackay, being in a wheelchair, had to be winched on board as there was no suitable alternative to the steps. On board there was no canteen, just a small bar for tea and coffee. As soon as the ship started to move, they closed the bar. It was a nice clear sunny day. The guy behind the bar told us when they were closing so we could get our drinks in before they shut. They gave us a deck of cards to play with so we wouldn't get bored because it was going to be a much longer journey than the one we had originally planned.

The vessel was designed mainly for truck drivers to board, go to their cabins and sleep rather than for tourists on holidays like the ferries we'd normally use. The passenger ferry would have travelled across the English Channel more quickly and taken a shorter route. The commercial ferry was slower because it had a heavier load, and it took a different route. We were on board for 8 hours. They let us rest on bunk beds in cabins whilst we were aboard. The bottom deck was filled with trucks, the next deck had cars and trucks. There was no lift, just steps. There were more decks for trucks and then came the cabins. They also transported a lot of fish. It was all you could smell. Everywhere!

When we finally got to our destination the Dutch team were waiting patiently. They greeted us enthusiastically, even though we were much later arriving than planned, smelling distinctively fishy as we got ashore. A delicious spread of meat, cheese, salad, (no fish!) and drinks was laid on at our host's cottage and we all chatted and laughed about our journey well into the night. Somehow, we still managed to play some solid badminton the next day and The Netherland's team members remain some of our best friends to this day.

If Dr Jim Mackay hadn't pushed us within disability badminton, it seems doubtful that the sport would be in the Paralympics in 2020/2021. He was one of the main driving forces within the sport of Para-Badminton. Jim first got involved by coming to help out at the Amputee Games in Stoke Mandeville. He was a wheelchair bound qualified doctor with a larger-than-life personality so he understood the classification system and things like that much better than we all did.

Jim became our self-appointed, unofficial England / GB Para-Badminton team manager and handled a lot of the administrative side of things such as hotel and flight bookings. He had a strong relationship with Badminton England, and that motivated us to keep pushing through the boundaries and hurdles wherever we found them. We appointed ourselves international players enthusiastically in an amateur, pioneering sort of way. All self-funded up to that point; if the other players thought you were good enough to play on their side and you had the money to cover your own travel and accommodation costs then you became part of 'the 5-man team.'

Even with the best people leading the way things didn't always go to plan. One year (1999) we competed in a tournament taking place in Israel. Off we went; Stuart, Jim, Colin Broadbridge, Julia, Tracey and me. All from Heathrow flying on different flights at different times. Had we all arranged to fly as a group this story may never have happened. Jim had organised the flight tickets and I was excited when they arrived in the envelope to the house. They were paper tickets that were posted out in a sleeve by the travel agent in those days, not like the direct purchase e-tickets that you get nowadays from numerous websites. Imagine my disappointment when I saw that they had spelt my name incorrectly. It didn't match the name on my passport so I would have been turned away at the check-in desk if I hadn't spotted the mistake in time!

We were due to compete fairly soon so I rang Jim, explained that the ticket was not valid, and he said he would get a replacement ticket sent out by post again. It meant that I ended up paying the full cost of two tickets instead of one which I wasn't happy about. To make up for the error, Jim said he'd look after my hotel bill, and we would sort out the difference when we came back from the competition. That was the deal as arranged before boarding the flight. When I got to the airport, I enjoyed the exciting feeling of adventure that started secretly creeping through my body as we landed at Tel-Aviv airport. I was in Israel, a country that was intriguing; in the mood to compete and win again. It was tantalising. I usually felt this way before a tournament but this one seemed even more special. Israel was a country that had a symbolic history for some of my friends from the Finchley / Barnet area.

We had a fantastic time at the tournament catching up with the regular competitors and settling old scores with our rivals. Everything was going really well, and I'd practically forgotten about the hiccup prior to the flight. It was as I was checking out of the hotel that I had a real shock. I went to the reception desk and stood in line chatting to everyone and wishing them all well until the next tournament. There was no Skype, Facebook, Instagram, Snapchat or Twitter in those days and telephone calls were expensive. Men are well known for not being great letter writers, so often the only time we did catch up was at international tournaments. During them we made sure that we exchanged enough gossip and camaraderie to see us through to the next tournament. It was soon my turn at the hotel reception desk. I handed over my key and said thank you to the receptionist as I'd had such a good time. Just as I turned to go, she called me back and handed me the bill for over £200, asking politely how I'd like to pay.

*'It's being paid by Dr Jim Mackay. We've been here for the badminton tournament and he said he would take care of the booking and payment.'*

I smiled at her in an understanding manner, thinking there had just been some sort of minor mix up in communication.

*'I'm sorry the bill hasn't been paid by Dr Jim Mackay. It's for you to settle at check out.'* she responded politely but firmly.

Well, I just stood there looking at her blankly. Back and forth the conversation went for a good few minutes with me insisting that it had all been arranged and paid for and her insisting that I had to pay. All the while the queue behind me was getting longer and longer with hotel guests starting to express their frustration at the situation. We all had planes to catch, places to be and none of us wanted to be held up along the way. I was trying my hardest not to lose my temper at the situation when along came one of the Dutch team on their way out. They saw me at reception looking totally harassed and fed up and asked me what the matter was. I told them what had happened.

*'I've been left in a sticky pickle by 'Dr Jam!'*

Jim's full name was James Mackay and when he met the Middle East badminton players they shortened 'James' to 'Jam' which he didn't like. He preferred using the short form 'Jim' but whenever we wanted to wind him up or tell him off, we called him 'Dr Jam.'

*'I don't have that sort of cash on me,'*

I explained, getting more upset by the minute. I was always careful about how much money I spent. I didn't use credit cards as it's too easy to simply overspend and get into lots of debt without being able to pay it back and I had a family to look after.

They made some enquiries and it turned out that Jim had no more money left to pay the hotel bill as he'd spent it all at the bar socialising on the previous night! After listening to my story, they suggested a solution would be for the Dutch team to pay my hotel bill via the Israeli Tournament Organising Committee. Then all I had to do was to pay the Dutch team back once I got home safely.

They really were such Good Samaritans that day, they were all concerned that I should make it safe and well back to my family. I agreed. It was a better proposition than being stranded in Israel, prosecuted, put into police custody or anything like that. I sat there wondering how I could possibly explain that one to Kamalpreet Kaur, ringing her from a police station in Tel Aviv? I don't think she would have been too impressed. Simply because of an administrative 'error/oversight' and a misspelled name on an airline ticket.

That's what good friends you make when you play a sport often and well. I had the utmost respect for them and was grateful that they offered to help me out. It's all about respect. Respecting yourself and being respected by those around you. When we returned to the UK, Jim sorted things out with the airline to get my double payment refunded and sent me the cheque and I promptly sent an international money order (cheque) to The Netherlands team in return.

It's something that we can all laugh about now but it was certainly a stressful experience and not at all funny at the time. Since then, I have always taken plenty of back up funds when I go abroad. 'You live and learn' as they say and that was certainly some lesson that I learned at the competition in Israel.

When you play badminton regularly with a club and start competing you come across the people who make sure all the rules are followed within the sport around the country. For us this is Badminton England. One year, as they were re-shaping the way they were organised, I decided I'd like to help England and join in with their efforts to get a 4 Nations championship organised for those with disabilities (England, Scotland, Wales, Northern Ireland) on an annual basis.

Clive Ellames was the Development Manager of Badminton England at that time, so I arranged a meeting and took him my paperwork to see what he thought about it. I wasn't too hopeful that he would even listen to my ideas but felt it best to give it a go. Nothing ventured, nothing gained' as they say. Badminton England is based in Milton Keynes, so I drove up, parked and went into reception. At the reception desk I was asked to sign in and when I mentioned that I was there to see Clive Ellames, they said he would come down to get me shortly. I just had time to have a quick look around the main reception area before he came over and took me to the bar where we ordered coffee and tea

'What is Badminton England doing to develop the disability side of the sport nationally?' I asked challengingly once we'd exchanged a little bit of small talk regarding the game, our families and other things.

He grinned at me and retorted, 'Why don't we see more Indian players and committee members leading the development of badminton in England?'

'Because our parents are too busy running shops and trying to educate their children. Who on earth has the time or energy after those long back-breaking hours to do any sports development' I snapped back angrily.

Now you'd think at this stage the conversation was going to end badly with me storming out in an offended huff or whatever. Instead, he looked straight at me trying to suppress a grin and calmly responded.

'What would **you** like to do to help **us** develop badminton further in England, Meva?'

Well I just looked at him wide-eyed, mouth open, and totally disbelieving at what I thought I'd just heard.

*'Are you serious?'* I asked him quietly, not daring to believe him. Had I misunderstood perhaps? But no, he really meant it. He suggested I come and view one meeting of the Development and Coaching Advisory Board to see what I thought of it. I went to a couple of meetings at the National Badminton Centre in Milton Keynes. It was because they got to know me and realised I had a contribution to make that I became a part of the Development and Coaching Advisory Board. That felt amazing as it meant I could really influence and shape what was going on in the sport I enjoyed playing so much.

And my time and effort wasn't wasted either. I managed to get them to agree to give 50% of the funding for 3 players to go to Thailand: myself, Antony Forster and Scott Richardson. I told them we wanted to go but we really couldn't do it without money. Because I was a grassroots player and of my experiences at the Israeli International tournament I could push for such things. On our return, I collected all the receipts from the players and handed them over to Derek Batchelor who ensured that the Badminton England Finance Department reimbursed us.

This arrangement went on for a couple of years but had to be stopped when more players wanted to join and because of a lack of available funding to ensure support for all of them. It was only when Lottery funding became available to enable support for elite Para-Badminton players with Paralympic medal potential that financial assistance was available again.

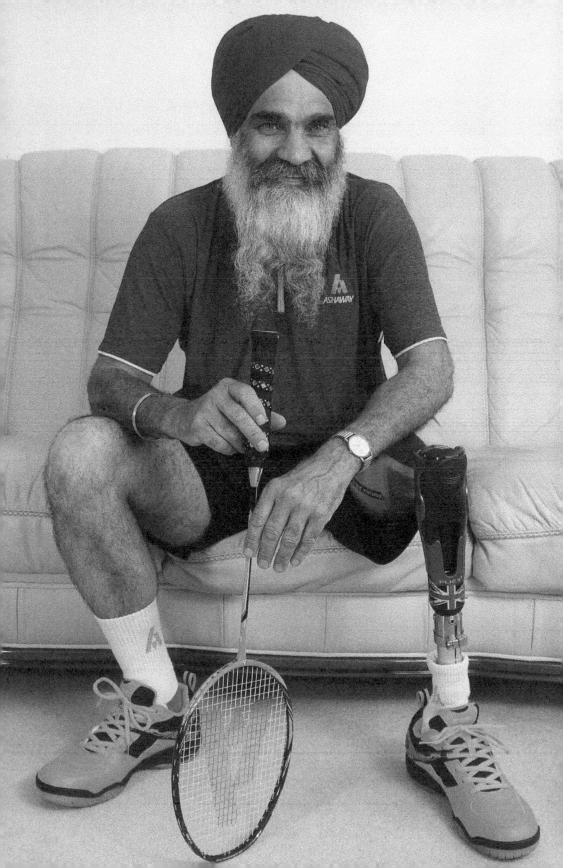

In the middle of a match in Thailand my partner, Scott Richardson of Pace Rehabilitation, looked down and asked, *'What's happened to your foot?'*

I went for a shot and landed my leg on the floor which made the foot twist. It was facing the wrong way so it perplexed him! Luckily, he had an Allen key set, because he is also a below knee amputee. He fixed it and we continued playing. Unfortunately, we lost but at least the Australian umpire, Kay Cody, allowed us extra time to fix the foot. Playing with the foot facing in the other direction hadn't damaged my game much. Nowadays I take a set of Allen keys with me everywhere I go. Scott Richardson played with us for around 2-3 years but has since moved on to golf. He was a pretty good player too, so it was a shame he didn't continue with badminton.

When we go to competitions it isn't all just about badminton. We make sure we have time to explore the area too. So, the next day Kay, Scott and I went to the shopping centre in a tuk tuk. We saw a place advertising 'foot massages' so, just for a laugh, I went over and asked how much and she told me. I showed her my prosthetic leg and asked cheekily,

*'one foot half price?'* nodding my head side to side as I spoke. She looked, laughed and replied, *'no, one foot more hard work. Double the price.'*

We all laughed at that and then went on our way around the shopping centre. In the evening, Scott decided it might be an idea to experience the local night clubs. I agreed to go with him, so we ordered a taxi and asked the driver to take us to one that he knew. The problem with just hopping into any taxi off the street is that they can try and cheat you. As Scott and I were chatting in the back we noticed we were passing the same buildings and streets three or four times and the taxi ride seemed to be lasting a long time even though the hotel was near the city centre. When we challenged him about it he stopped at a very seedy looking place and said we'd arrived. We didn't like the look of it at all, so we told him, *'we're not getting out here, mate. Take us to a better club.'*

Well the next place he took us to wasn't much better but we got out and went inside. As we stood by the bar Scott looked at me and grinned.

*'What do you think about all the ladies in here then, Meva?'*

*'They're not bad looking are they?'* I replied and at that he burst out laughing.

*'Take another look. Ever seen a lady with a large Adam's apple?'* he smirked.

And when I looked closer, I saw what he meant. We were in a 'lady boys' club where the men dress and look like women. And some of them were very convincing! Well, as we'd already put our drinks order in, we quickly gulped them down and scampered out of there back to the hotel.

Over breakfast the next day the Indian team heard we'd been out clubbing and asked if I'd take them there. I agreed but didn't tell them about our actual experience once inside. One of the guys in their team was in a wheelchair which we wouldn't have been able to get into the taxi or into the club. We pretended to him that we weren't going and after dinner he went to bed.

Once he'd gone, we headed off to the club and I bought them the first round of drinks. Whilst we were there, the 'ladies' started to come over to us asking us to buy drinks for them too. Now it turns out that if you keep buying them drinks, they ask if you'd like to come into the back room with them and that's where you find out that they're not girls, but boys! Not that any of us stuck around that long. The Indian team enjoyed the night out with me, but the wheelchair guy was really annoyed at us at breakfast the next morning when he found out that we'd gone without him!

I don't drink alcohol and in Thailand there is not much vegetarian food on offer. Their main diet is mostly fish, meat, plain rice, boiled rice and sauce. When you have a limited choice you simply make do. My diet wasn't the best during our time away for that tournament; two days were spent travelling to Thailand and back, we had one competition classification and practise day, and the tournament matches took place over 4-5 days.

Thailand were the hosts for the 6th World Para-Badminton Championships that year and it was the first time that all para-badminton players received a compulsory international licence number to compete. SL2AD-ENG, International Badminton Association for the Disabled (IBAD) was mine. SL2 meant standing lower category, (amputee) and A meant above knee whereas B meant below knee. The classification categories for para-badminton players have grown a lot since then.

Para-badminton players from all the other countries stayed at the same hotel so they used to arrange parties and informal get-togethers after the matches. Hotel drink prices are sky high so luckily there was a local shop around the corner which was also an off-licence. Most nights, after our evening meal, we would put chairs out in front of the hotel. One of the players would head over to the shop and get some supplies and we would all sit around, drinking and chatting well into the night. It was always warm, dry and pleasant sitting outside together. There were players from Australia, The Netherlands, Germany and England socialising. We were friends as well as competitors.

## ∾ Friends Club Together ∾

When you join a badminton club and grow with it over a long time because you live and work in the area, you get the opportunity to be more involved in club activities. In all my years in badminton I've had the chance to take on roles such as match secretary, treasurer, team captain and gone on to run my own clubs with other players. I've sorted out match fixtures, picked up and dropped off players and generally had a lot of fun and enjoyment getting involved wherever and whenever I could. I made the most of it because I enjoyed the game so much. Setting up a new type of badminton club that caters for disabled and able-bodied players of all ages doesn't always go smoothly. Badminton clubs need venues, and the management staff of those venues have to be very supportive of such initiatives.

In 2005 I tried to set up the Burnt Oak and Barnet Badminton Club which integrated amputee players with able-bodied players in one club. We also entered a team in the Enfield Men's Four League. 2005 was the year that Frank Gardener returned to work for the BBC as Security Correspondent in a wheelchair and using a frame following his spinal injury in 2004, received whilst working on a War on Terror reporting assignment in the Middle East. Disability and the issues facing disabled people became very relevant that year in London and the fight to stop terrorist attacks in the UK was high on the agenda.

We had amputees and people with learning disabilities coming to our club. Barnet Council generously granted us funding of £6000 towards coaching and court costs but Burnt Oak leisure management would not take the cheque which caused us some concern. The funding instructions from Barnet Council clearly stated that it had to be used by April and we only found out in late March that Burnt Oak leisure management would not accept it. Consequently, we had to give the cheque back to Barnet Council and find another way to fund the club. It was so important that the Leisure Centre accepted payment so that the funding could be shown to have been utilised properly and would have had a chance of continuing for future years. By giving the cheque back it affected the concept negatively and made it more difficult to apply for other support from Barnet Council for anything else we wanted to develop within the club

We only lasted 2 years there because of difficulties obtaining proper paperwork regarding the breakdown of expenditure for the club from the management staff along with other issues. It was a very sad day when we finally had to make the tough decision to close. I really felt it because I had put so much effort into trying to make it work. It took me a while to get over the pain of closure. It was something that initially I couldn't accept but eventually realised that it was inevitable, and that it simply hadn't been the right time for me to undertake such a venture. Overall, it was a very good learning experience, dealing with all the external and internal politics and the next time I attempted to set up a club I was much better prepared.

It took us until 2012 to finally get a brand-new club up and running. It was called the Herts Toppers Badminton Club which integrated disabled players with able-bodied players. The success of the Paralympics in London 2012 certainly made us feel that something had changed regarding the attitude of many in the population to disabled sports people. Gobi Ranganathan, Martin Rooke and I started the initiative off. Martin and Gobi are both excellent wheelchair badminton players, so we worked well as a team together. After creating the club, we decided to enter it in the South West Herts Badminton Independent League where we would be playing matches against able-bodied players. This had never before occurred in the UK. We were also the first club to have more than one disabled person playing in an able-bodied league.

Herts Toppers Badminton Club has been running well from 2012 to the present (2022). It's taken a lot of energy to get the club to where it is now. Our league results have been impressive. 2012-2013 was our first competitive season in the league and we came 5th overall. Every year since then we have improved our results. In 2015-2016 we finished top of the league with an unbeaten 9 wins and 1 draw. We played 140 games that year, winning 100 while losing only 40. We came top of the league again in 2018-2019 and we started 2019-2020 in second place until all badminton competition came to a premature halt because of the coronavirus restrictions.

In every match we made sure we had one disabled player in our team. Either in a wheelchair or standing. Our youngest player is just 14 years old. It's an honour to be able to name some of them here: Duncan Williams, Dave Marshall, Birinder Singh Dhesi (my son), Sunny Ward, Charlie Corke, his sister Lillie Corke, Martin Rooke (club captain) and Gobi Ranganathan (chairman).

It gives me such pleasure to see the next generation of badminton players going on to achieve some of the things that we helped develop. And if during my time with them I can inspire some competitive spirit and teamwork, just as others have in me, then I will feel really proud. That is a feeling almost better than winning a tournament yourself. That is why I have stayed and played one sport for so long. Anyone can do things for themselves but to do something for others is more important.

*Martin Rooke, Tokyo Para-Badminton Paralympian and Member of HertsToppers Badminton Club*

## by Ergun Ahmed

I am known to my friends as Ergi and am married to a beautiful Japanese woman named Terujo.

We have 2 daughters. I was a drummer in a Japanese Rock 'n' Roll band, regularly touring America, Europe and Scandinavia in my younger days. When I wasn't touring or playing in gigs and concerts I would be working as an Events Manager for a busy events company. I led a hectic and busy lifestyle before being struck down by an infectious illness, Pneumococcal Septicaemia, in December 2005.

I was rushed to hospital where my body went into septic shock with multiple organ failure and the doctors put me in an induced coma. 15 days later I woke up in ICU in the Royal Free Hospital to find that I'd had both legs below the knee amputated. My feet had become necrotic and couldn't be saved. I had also been fitted with a tracheostomy. My two young children, (Yuhmi was 5 and Reina was coming up to her 2nd birthday), were not allowed to visit me until I came out of ICU and had been transferred to another ward. I didn't see them until mid-January 2006 as the doctors thought it would be too scary and psychologically disturbing for them.

By April 2006 I was being fitted with prosthetics and had intense physiotherapy for 2 years. Within the first few months of physiotherapy, I built up enough confidence to try walking outside. I used to put my prosthetic legs and walking sticks in a bag which Terujo had made specially to hang on the back of my wheelchair so that I could wheel myself to nearby Hampstead Heath. There I would put my legs on and practice walking. When you are walking outside no ground is level and you really notice this when you walk with prosthetics. I would end up looking at the ground with my head down most of the time because of that.

I had to overcome this and learn to look ahead in the normal way when walking so Terujo and I thought it was a good idea to join a leisure centre and try out badminton. We hoped it would encourage me to look up at the shuttlecock and find my footing while not concentrating on my legs. We made a point of going once and sometimes twice a week and loved playing the game. We started inviting friends to join in our badminton games and with every session I would get more confident with my legs. I found my steps became more natural. My leg muscles built up to become more nimble, which in turn made it easier in my everyday life. I found badminton to be a really great form of rehabilitation in my struggles after becoming disabled. This is where my badminton story begins.......

## Meva

I was at the limb centre in Stanmore, sitting in the men's fitting room waiting for my prosthetist to bring back my leg after servicing it when in came this young guy who introduced himself as Ergun, a double below knee amputee. He was there because of a re-cast for his prosthetics. As most amputees do when they are in fitting rooms together, we started chatting. (Because we all know we are in this together and are going to go through many of the same issues; having to confront the same problems all the time). I felt a bit uncomfortable at first because he kept looking very intently at me and then, as if he had a light bulb moment, leant in closer towards me and asked:

*'Hey, you're the guy in the poster on the noticeboard outside aren't you? The one about the disability badminton club?'*

'Yes, am I that easy to recognise?' I answered, relieved that was why he was looking at me so keenly and pleased that someone had taken notice of the poster. I had only asked the limb centre to put it up there a couple of weeks ago. I had just set up the Wednesday night disability badminton group at Burnt Oak Leisure Centre which played between 5pm-7pm and was always on the lookout for members to join. We didn't have to be members of Badminton England for the disability coaching sessions but if you wanted to play with the able-bodied club members after 7pm you had to be considered good enough to play with them and be a member of Badminton England.

Laughing he said, *'I play badminton regularly with my wife and friends. I am new to the disability world so I didn't know how to meet people who face the same difficulties as me.'*

*'Yes, it's more than possible,"* I responded. *'The trick is not to look down at the ground and at your prosthetics, but always look up instead. Focus on the shuttle and your legs / feet will move with you. Like this,'*

I said and stood up, pretending that I had a badminton racquet in my hand and moved around the fitting room as if I was on the badminton court playing a match.

He was keen to know more and took down the details of the club. The only trouble was that he lived in Hampstead Heath and didn't drive, so to come to Burnt Oak Leisure Centre he would have to travel roughly an hour in each direction.

## Ergun Ahmed

I would walk 5 minutes, get the 68 bus to Belsize Park Station, then get the Northern Line train to Burnt Oak Station then another bus to the leisure centre. I was very keen to play in a club, especially one that was for amputees. I pre-arranged with Meva that I would come on his nights.

## Meva

When he turned up at the club, I took him through the basic orientation session., introducing him to other club members, sorting out membership forms and showing him the first few easy shots and moves around the court. In just 6 to 8 months of playing badminton he started to get really good. And he was getting good enough to compete in a few of the local tournaments too. Ergun went on to play in 4 Nations' competitions in Largs in Scotland, Cardiff in Wales, and some friendly matches at Imperial College in London. He would even come down and help me coach new amputees at LimbPower Amputee Games weekends at Stoke Mandeville.

One Wednesday evening at Burnt Oak, (he must have been at the club almost a year by that time), we had just come to the end of the disability session. It was 7 p.m. and Ergun started to pack up to head off home. I waved goodbye to him and carried on coaching 2 players who had learning disabilities. There were 4 badminton courts in the hall. I was on court 2 with two boys showing them easy forehand / backhand drills.

The able-bodied members of the club usually started coming on court and playing once the disability session was finished. This evening, 3 players saw Ergun heading off court 1 and called to him, asking if he would like to be the 4th player in their men's doubles game. Ergun had just finished 2 hours of badminton with us, but he was as keen as I was in my early days to play and keep playing so naturally he said 'yes'. So, there he was, the only disabled player, with 3 able-bodied team mates giving each point his best attempt.

## Ergun Ahmed

I was playing doubles with the able-bodied team and paired with Ade, the star player, very fast and very light on his feet. He was covering the back of the court while I was covering the front near the net. We had a few fast rallies and were leading. On this particular shot the shuttle came to the right of me where I thought I could reach and get the shot back, but my legs just weren't fast enough. I kept my eye on the shuttle still to the side of me and as it went past, Ade realised I could not reach it. So, he dashed across, took the shot quite low to the ground, sweeping it quickly upwards in a full power forehand drive which hit my eye - SMACK! - full on in the middle. I didn't even have time to blink it was that fast! I was knocked down to the floor and could not see a thing out of it. When I tried to open it, it was filled with blood.

## Meva

I was just finishing off my session on my court with the 2 youngsters when I heard a loud, terrifying scream coming from Ergun's court. Everyone in the hall heard it. They turned to see what had happened. I dashed over to find out what the commotion was all about and when I got to their court my heart froze. All I could see was Ergun sitting on the court floor, holding his hands around his eye and moaning in pain. It was excruciating.

*'What happened?'*

*'The shuttle,' answered one of the other players. 'Went straight in his eye.' Quick get the first aiders, call the manager. Oh my God, it's ok. It's ok, Ergun. We will sort it. Don't worry.'*

*'How?'*

*'It was dreadful, it all happened so quickly.'*

There was a lot of running up and down corridors to get the right staff and when they saw what had happened, they immediately called for an ambulance. Ergun's eye was deeply bloodshot and he was in an incredible amount of pain. The hard, leather covered cork base of the shuttle had impacted into his right eye at a tremendous pace. As fast as a bullet.

We were all terribly worried and in shock. Ergun's team members who had been on court with him all felt so guilty about what had happened. Each club night after that evening was a tense affair with everyone being very careful on court. We waited in agony and suspense for news of Ergun and what we could all do to help his recovery. Accidents do happen on court, but I'd never seen anything like this. It was a time I will never forget. There was a sober atmosphere when the ambulance came and took him off to Moorfields Eye Hospital for a thorough investigation into the injury.

Whenever there are major incidents on court involving players in a Badminton England Affiliated Club, Badminton England needs to be informed so that they can investigate any liability and insurance issues. The Leisure Centre management also wanted a full report on what had happened.

I rang Badminton England the very next day and told them about the accident. As I was a coach, I had liability insurance with Badminton England and wanted to know where I stood with the situation. If I had to take responsibility for the incident, then having the insurance cover to help with any costs for Ergun's recovery would make it all much easier to deal with. I was feeling upset enough about the whole incident as it was. It would have been far worse if there had been no support at all out there. They asked me about Ergun's membership form, and I said that he had definitely filled one out and paid the fee. They couldn't find any trace of his membership application and that held up matters no end. I made enquiries at Burnt Oak Leisure Centre, and it turned out that the manager at the time had those forms just sitting on his desk! He'd had them for 3 months and hadn't forwarded them on to Badminton England. It didn't take long for the senior management of the leisure centre to transfer that manager out of there after that.

Ergun ended up having a very difficult 5-6 months because of the eye injury. He had to have two operations as he had sustained retinal damage and lens scarring. His eyesight took a long time to improve, and we worried for so long that he might go blind in that eye. He had a lot to deal with in such a very short time. First the amputations and recovery from them and now, just a year or so later, a major eye injury. It was a very stressful time for him, his wife and his two young children.

## Ergun Ahmed

I play badminton occasionally but not in any competitive capacity. I play for leisure only with my wife Tejuro and our friends. I am working full time as a skilled gardener at one of The Royal Parks, Richmond Park at The Isabella Plantation. I moved to Leyton East London with my wife and daughters.

I cycle with an electric bicycle to work and back which is a great way of keeping fit as it is around a 45-mile round trip. I have also taken up drumming again as a hobby and to challenge my coordination. I joined a band who occasionally go to Europe to play shows and concerts and also occasional London shows. It's a great hobby for an ageing man....

# Chapter 4
# Do You Want to Join a White Man's Club?

*'Hey, Meva. Did y' hear, lunchtime clubs are back on again next Monday,'* one of my school friends said to me as we sat finishing our lunch in the canteen.

*'What are lunchtime clubs?'* I asked unenthusiastically.

I'd just had lesson after lesson all morning and wasn't really that keen to do more lessons in the lunchtime. With only one afternoon of PE to look forward to all week, clubs weren't that high on my list of priorities. Especially if it was just more of the same thing. Teacher talks, we listen, and pretend we like learning what they have to teach. Try not to yawn, not to lose concentration, not to get bored, not to stare out the window, not to fidget, and most difficult of all, not to throw paper missiles at each other when the teacher isn't looking.

We had a few boys in the school who were more bullies than others. When we played cricket, they would throw the ball directly at you; a hard cork ball. They were white, older and bigger than us so they would always pick on us Indians as there weren't many of us in the class.

One of them was surprised many years later when I knocked on his door to pick up his sister for a Christmas party. He recognised me and said, *'You can't come to my house, it's my party.'*

'I've only come to pick up your sister,' I said calmly.

'How do you know my sister?' he barked back angrily.

'She comes to my shop, the greengrocers. I know your sister's daughter as well'

I replied with a smirk on my face relishing the obvious discomfort it was causing him. He still had the same attitude towards foreigners as he'd had when he was a boy in our school. He was never going to change.

When I first went to Alder Boy's school I couldn't speak English so one of the Indian boys taught me how to say 'good morning' to the teacher, (or so I thought). I trusted him because he was Indian and assumed he would look after me, but I soon found out that he had a wicked sense of humour. My only experience of school prior to this was going with my cousin to his school for a short time. We did everything together, so I didn't think about making friends on my own until I started at Alder.

This Indian boy showed me how to put two fingers up (in a V sign) each time the teacher called my name for registration in the morning. Being new in the school and not knowing anything different, that's what I did. And every single time I did it, I'd get put in the corner with my face to the wall in humiliation and not know why. I was learning about friendship the hard way. All the other children in the class thought it was really funny the first couple of times. This went on for around 2 weeks until one of my newly made English friends told me I was actually swearing at the teacher! Needless to say, I soon stopped greeting adults that way and my new friend and I laid into the guy who'd got me into trouble and taught him a bit of a lesson too.

I was a teenager at a typical boys' school, so we had a choice of chess club, book club, music club or badminton club. The only one I thought I might like the sound of was the badminton club. So the next week I went over to take a look. The badminton court was set up in the assembly hall, a high ceiling church hall with high beams and a stage at the back. We used it for school plays, PE and assembly in the morning. We would sit on benches and the teachers would sit on chairs on the stage.

When I got there, I saw a couple of the older boys were in the middle of playing the game. I watched for a bit. It looked quite appealing the way they were serving, reaching for the plastic shuttle with their racquets and sometimes hitting it over or, more often, straight into the net. I asked if I could play with them.

*'Have you played this game before?'* the taller of the two boys asked.

*'No,'* I replied excitedly. *'I've only just discovered it. Looks like fun though and I'd love to learn how to play it.'*

They looked at each other, then at me and said, *'You have to learn how to play first. We can't teach you the game. We only play.'*

I left a little downhearted at that. What now? It looked like a really fun game but who could teach me to play? As we waited for the next lesson to start (the teacher was always a little delayed for the first lesson after the lunch break) I told my friends all about this game; badminton.

The only boy interested was Manjit Singh so the following week we both quickly finished our lunch and raced over to the court early so we could play before anyone else got there. We didn't know how to hold the racquet, how to hit the shuttle or how to score a point but we had a lot of fun and made it all up. It was frustrating and exciting all at the same time trying to figure out how to actually play properly.

We weren't on the court that long before the other two boys came over. They asked us to get off the court so they could play and we both said, *'No, we were here first and we want to play.'*

As you can imagine, this led to a big argument. We knew at the time the two older boys were a senior prefect and head boy and they could have made life difficult for us by giving us detention or other punishments. But that still didn't stop us standing our ground. Luckily, before the situation got too out of hand, the deputy headmaster came over and asked what we were arguing about. Manjit and I both said, *'They won't let us play. It is a lunchtime club, and we want to play. Lunchtime clubs are supposed to be open clubs where anyone can play.'*

The two older boys replied that because we didn't know how to play the game it would not be much fun playing with us. Saying something like that to me was like showing a guard dog a burglar to chase! I was so worked up that Manjit Singh and I ended up challenging them to a proper match in 4 weeks' time. That would show them who knows how to play, I thought.

'*Senior boys, do you accept the challenge?*' boomed the deputy headmaster's voice loudly around the court in an official manner. (He'd been in the British Army in the Punjab, India so had that military style when he talked.) They both looked at each other, had a quick whispered chat and then said that they did. They thought because they were bigger than us and had been playing for longer it would be an easy win for them.

And that was that. Manjit Singh and I now had a big mission ahead of us — to win our very first badminton match when we didn't even know how to play and knew no one who could teach us the game! No pressure then. When the shock of what we'd just done finally wore off we quickly got into action.

We had a really nice caretaker, Mr Davies, in our school. Manjit and I used to help him keep the school yard tidy by putting all the rubbish in the bins during break times. Having talked everything over, we decided to tell him all about our little challenge and what difficulties we were in as we didn't have anywhere to play. He looked at us thoughtfully, rubbed his chin, filled his pipe, fiddled with his flat cap after taking it off his head, and said, '*what about you boys practsin' after school whilst the cleaners are in?*' Once they finish you have to go, the place 'as to be fully locked up. I'll clear it wit' the headmaster. Shouldn' be no probl'm seein' as deputy head knows 'bout it.'

We couldn't believe our luck! He was happy for us to play for an hour or so up to 3 or 4 times a week if we wanted to. And for one of the cleaners, it proved to be helpful too. Her daughter was in my sister's school and would come to our school whilst her mum did the cleaning. Normally she would be sitting on her own getting bored but now we were playing badminton after school she had some company. Not that she played with us though. She would just sit and do her homework or help out with scoring and refereeing if we asked her to. We're all still good friends after all these years. She works in the local Waitrose in Whetstone, so I still see her now and again.

Unknown to the head boy and senior prefect, we were playing badminton after school 3-4 times a week. We couldn't stay later than 5pm and had to race home before our mums got back from work. Otherwise, they might think we'd had to stay behind at school because we'd been naughty and had detention. And that would have meant getting into more trouble with our parents. We didn't want that because we had an important badminton match to win!

Those 4 weeks passed incredibly quickly. When it was time, we approached the two seniors and asked them for a match. The deputy headmaster was there as an observer to ensure fair play, but we did our own scoring. The first game went quickly and they won it without even breaking into a sweat. Boy, did we have to think hard how to get back and win the second game to stay in with a chance. That second game turned out to be a really close one. We had a good plan on how to play and we were both fired up to win. No way were we going to lose the challenge that we had set ourselves. The third and final game we won easily.

We focused on strategy more than strength, finding their weaknesses during the earlier games and exploiting those. We lost the first game because we were lobbing high to them. They were both quite tall and could reach those shots easily. So we changed tactics by hitting low with good serves and that made them work harder. We forced them to play our way. After that match, there were no more problems about us playing with them at the lunchtime badminton club.

In my final year in school, just before New Year, the school officer, Mr Morley, asked me if I wanted to join his badminton club on a Monday evening at St Martin's School. It was a session only for adults but as I was in my final year I was seen as an adult. It was one that you could only get recommended for and I had to cycle there. It was at least a mile away from my house. I jumped at the chance. I wanted to keep playing, keep improving my game and being asked to play with the adults made me feel really proud.

I went for a few weeks and a lady named Barbara Jenkins played with me and saw something in me. She asked if I wanted to join another club in Finchley Central which met on Tuesday nights, called Gainsborough. It was very near my house.

Her words were *'if you want to join a white man's club.'*

I asked why it was called 'a white man's club' and she said because the badminton kit of real players was all white.

Of course, I wanted to join! But there was just one problem. Every bit of my kit was black; shorts, plimsolls, all the school uniform kit was black, not white. So what now? It took me around 4 weeks to pluck up the courage to ask my parents for money for the kit. In those days we didn't have lots of money and no one ever asked for anything because it wasn't the done thing. We decided that I would help pay for the kit with the money I earned from my weekend job at the greengrocers. £2.50 if I helped out at the greengrocers after school or £3.00 for all day Saturday. If I worked Sunday mornings from 9am-1pm I'd earn 10 bob (50p). I wasn't serving customers, just cleaning up the shop and filling shelves. Once I started serving customers my wages went up.

Mostly, I got paid in old money. There used to be 240 pennies in one pound. Since decimalisation in 1971 there are only 100 pennies in one pound. Most of the old coins like shillings, florins, half crowns, threepenny bits and halfpenny pieces were taken out of circulation that year. But it took us all a long while to get used to it and we would often say 'hay'penny, thruppeny bit, shilling' even after the new coins came in. The sixpence (often referred to as a 'tanner') was finally taken out of circulation in 1980 so that gives you some idea of how long it took people to get used to the change from the old money to decimal coinage.

Usually, my wages from the newspaper round and the greengrocers went towards helping my mum with everyday family bills. She would give me pocket money out of that. But now, we put aside a little bit from that each week to save up for my white badminton kit, so I could join 'the white man's club'. She couldn't buy everything at once, so she bought one thing at a time. Which felt like ages for someone impatient to have it all yesterday!

I was itching to join the new club and didn't know how I would be able to wait until I finally had all the kit. Eventually, I got my white T shirt, white V-neck, white shorts, white socks and Green Flash Dunlop trainers. The shorts came down to my knees and the socks were the nice long ones, not ankle socks. Everything was made from cotton, all well made. And I wanted a new racquet as I only used the ones from the school, so I worked at the greengrocers and put money aside for that too.

When I got to the club I had a real shock. Everyone was much older than I, and they were playing with real feather shuttles not plastic like the ones at our school. Bankers, lawyers, school teachers and other professionals were all playing badminton to help release the stress and tension of their working lives. They were very sociable, and everyone used to stop for tea and biscuits at 10pm. The club ran from 7pm-11pm. There was only one court in the church hall. They didn't want too many members as there was not enough court space, so you had to get there early in order to get a game. In those days badminton was always played in church halls, not a sports hall. The nearest place that had the luxury of 3 courts to play on was the Orion Hall on Stamford Hill.

To be a recognised member of the club you had to play for 3 weeks and then the committee would decide whether you could be a member or not. I really wanted to keep playing so when they put me against one of the committee members I made sure I worked really hard during the game. In the third week I was really tense, my palms were sweating and my throat was dry as they turned round to me and said, *'you're okay,'* (which was their way of saying that they thought I was good enough to play with them!)

You couldn't take the grin off my face for days afterwards. I was so happy to be part of a proper membership badminton club. I went around telling everyone. My family, the Lesters, neighbours, school friends, in fact, anyone who would listen. Especially as I had worked so hard to help buy the kit and played the best that I possibly could for weeks and weeks.

It was all a very sociable experience. Jim Grayson was our chairman at Gainsborough and Colin Pearson was the treasurer because in his day job he was a bank manager. Jim always used to bring us beer and Coca Cola to drink during the break. He had the keys to lock up (because it was a church hall) and sometimes he would let us play late, (until well after midnight) and then go to work the next day!

There was another badminton club in the area at Long Lane. It was a sort of youth club where young Indian boys and girls played the game. One of the guys who played at that club started working at the same greengrocers as I and invited me to play with them one evening. His name was Iqbal Choughley, but at the greengrocers we nicknamed him Charlie. He went by the name of Charlie Choughley for many years.

I went there a few times. It was a bit of a culture shock compared to Gainsborough. In the Gainsborough Club it was all older professional people, bankers, accountants, solicitors and estate agents who were naturally reserved, mild mannered and very English. In Long Lane, it was the total opposite. Lots of energetic and enthusiastic youngsters who were very vocal and extremely keen, but they only had plastic shuttlecocks and cheap racquets to play with compared to the high-end racquets and real feather shuttlecocks that Gainsborough used. The system these youngsters used and how they picked the games and players were a big challenge for me to understand. Charlie Choughley turned out to be a very good player, so I asked him if he'd like to join 'the white man's club'.

He hesitated at first because of the cost of getting the kit. Eventually he said yes so I asked the club members if I could bring a guest.

*'Is he any good?'* they asked.

*'Well he's young and I think he's better than me,'* I replied, which seemed to do the trick.

He came and within two weeks he was accepted into the club. He was a big guy, had a very good backhand smash, strong and a good mover on the court. In badminton he's only ever known as Charlie, it's how he's recognised. Only his wife insists on us calling him Iqbal. Charlie and I were men's doubles partners in quite a few tournaments over the years. Even before losing my leg and after losing my leg as well. He stopped playing badminton in the late 1990s after getting married and having a family. Charlie had a greengrocer shop just like I did in the 1980s, but this also had to close. And his next job left him no time to play badminton anymore.

Colin Pearson, our treasurer, was one of the youngest there and initially joked, *'no we don't want another one like you mate'* with a twinkle in his eye and a smirk on his face when I mentioned Charlie to them. But when he came, and Colin saw him play he said he would always have Charlie Choughley on his team so he could win all the matches. Being the younger members of the club, we really felt ready to compete. There were around half a dozen of us who were good enough and interested in playing matches. The nearest league we could put our club into was Barnet. Luckily for us they said we could join. We had a chance to play in a medley of men's, ladies' and mixed doubles. It was great for us because it meant we got to play 9 matches.

In that first season I really had fun. I played for two different clubs in the same league, different divisions and no one found out as I was a total unknown at that time. There were two groups, A and B. As it was a medley you could end up playing 2 men's and 1 mixed doubles. You had to be very fit to want to play so many matches, and I did that not just once, but twice! I would play in Group A under my name Meva Singh and in Group B I'd use my initials and surname M S Dhesi.

Charlie Choughley and I were so new, and no one expected anyone to be so keen on playing badminton that they would want to play so many matches, so we got away with it. It was only because Flying Feathers won the league that they noticed I was named as a player on the winning side. I could have been banned or thrown out of both clubs if they hadn't accepted that I didn't know it wasn't allowed to play for more than one club in the league.

Getting to all the different matches wasn't easy. We were lucky as Jim Grayson would offer to take us to them in his car right over to Stamford Hill which was at least 8 or 9 miles away. In the second season at Gainsborough, we had a Christmas party organised by Jim Grayson to which the Hadley Badminton Club members were invited. It was designed to be a fun night; everyone was asked to dress up and bring a bottle.

We were going to play badminton in our fancy dress that night. It was the first English party I had been to, and I took along a bottle of whisky. I had fairly long hair at the time. We all had a few drinks (everyone basically drinking what they had brought along and sharing it around the group if they had brought a big bottle). I went into the kitchen to get a top up and two of the older women players were there chatting when I walked in.

*Hey Meva, are you growing your hair to be a girl now?'* one of them asked me. I was a little drunk at the time (this was one of the only times I've ever drunk alcohol, so it went straight to my head).

*'I'd make a really pretty girl. I could win lots of the women's league badminton matches as well. That would be cool!'* I retorted laughing as I said it. Next thing I knew they were putting lipstick on me, tying my hair back in a ponytail, dressing me up as a schoolgirl with a badminton skirt borrowed from one of the other female players and for the rest of the night that is how I stayed. There was no mistletoe at the party but because Charlie and I were the two youngest male players in the club, we still got some kisses from the older married women

There were quite a lot of photographs taken of that night. Jim had asked one of the players, Len Newson, to act as the official cameraman because he had his own darkroom at home. (There were no digital cameras or mobile phones with cameras in those days). A week or two later the photographs appeared at the club and caused a lot of hilarity and comments. Len Newson told us that his son had actually noticed the photograph of me dressed like a schoolgirl and had pointed it out to him at the breakfast table. Of course, he brought them in for the rest of the club members to enjoy. We shared a lot of laughter at the club. It wasn't always about competing and winning.

At that party one of the top players, Stepan Bedrossian, asked if Charlie and I wanted to join Hadley Badminton Club. By now I was already playing for Gainsborough and Flying Feathers in Finchley. Out of curiosity, we went to the summer clubs that they held at Stamford Hill organised by the Hadley Badminton Club. The summer season ran from April to August and taking part in the summer season didn't automatically guarantee you entry into the winter season at a club.

At one point I was playing badminton 4-6 times a week depending on how many matches were on. And club nights were at least 3 times a week. I had no social life outside of badminton, it was the only thing I wanted to do. I was really enjoying playing for three clubs and worked towards getting my coaching badge.

I had no particular reason to do so. I'd seen the badge on the coaches at the different clubs and it looked really nice so I wanted one too! Well, why else would you want to be a coach? Seemed a good enough reason to me at the time. The course took 10 weeks to complete at evening classes. They covered the laws, regulations, how to play the different strokes and lots of essential practical things that coaches should know. There was an exam at the end, and when I passed and received my coaching badge, I was over the moon.

There were some real characters at the badminton clubs. Dick Kent of Hadley (Middlesex County Player) and Brian Elliott of Flying Feathers (badminton coach - one of the best at the time) were particularly memorable because they would wind me up a lot before starting to play. These guys were really serious about the game, took no prisoners and always played to win.

Dick Kent and I really got on well with each other. He would always challenge me to do those shots that I couldn't do well. I learnt so much from him because of that. He could lose his temper easily on court with his partner or the opposition if they didn't listen to him. He would wind up the opposition before the game started. That was his strategy. He would find your weakness very quickly. He read the game very well. I am just like him now and I do exactly the same to wind people up, speeding the game up, slowing the game down. I learnt all that from Dick Kent.

Brian Elliott could be quite negative about foreigners, so I always thought he didn't like me because I was Indian. It was only when I was in hospital after I lost my leg and Brian Elliott was one of the first visitors who came to see me that I learnt the truth. That was his strategy. Brian always looked for a weakness in his opponent and mine was the fact that I was Indian so if he said negative things about foreigners or Indians of course it wound me up or upset me. If you wind up someone then they can't concentrate on the game so it's easier to win.

But he told me as I lay on the hospital bed after losing my leg, *'That's badminton, it's part of the game. On the court we are opponents and out to win. Off the court Meva, we are friends and I want you to get well enough to play with us again.'*

That was when I understood. On the court it doesn't matter who you are, you are serious and giving 100%. It can go badly or well. When you come off the court, you shake hands and it's all forgotten. You're friends. It's finished. If they've cheated you, good luck to them. If they keep cheating you, do it back to them in a way they won't forget. Do it purposely. The main thing is to know that cheating is no good. You should always try to win fair and square. Sport is about people; you make so many friends socially. If you are a fair player, they remember you. If you cheat, they remember you too. But for the wrong reason.

My winning streak and determination to play well came from Brian Elliott. He was a really good coach. Although I have never been coached by him, I've learnt things by playing against him in tournaments and at the Flying Feathers during club nights. He always challenged us to work harder at the game. To be the best. He was a much better player and didn't like losing to us, so it always made us try hard to beat him. Mike Goodwin, Middlesex County coach and Hadley badminton club member, was also a very good level 2 coach. He was very tall, an older man, friendly, but also aggressive at times. He always tried to get the best out of you, and sometimes he would be purposefully aggressive to test a player's temperament and courage. I've been on the receiving end of that aggressive streak from him too.

One week, there was a particular backhand sliced shot that he asked everyone to do. Some could do it, but I couldn't. No matter how hard I tried. I simply wasn't getting it. At the end of the session he turned to me and said, *'Meva, by next week make sure you can do it or go home and don't come back to another session.'*

He sounded really angry, so I decided to take him at his word and not fail. Anyone else being spoken to like that might have been scared to attend the next session but not me. The following week I came back, and he put me against the England champion Gillian Gilks. She was a very good badminton player, a multi-medal winner and had excellent placement. Mike used to coach her at one stage in her badminton career. Now they are happily married. They are both still very good friends of mine. She hit the shot at me, and I sliced it back perfectly.

Mike came over with a big grin on his face and said, *'Well done, why couldn't you do that last week?'*

He always helped me to play my best game wherever we went. When I acquired my coaching badge, he was the instructor and examiner. He would coach us for ten weeks on how to be a coach and then test us. He was a strict but fair examiner. Gillian Gilks is no pushover on the badminton court. She initially came to help Mike out on the coaching course to develop our shots, like the backhand slice. At the time she was a member of the Hadley club as well. When she first joined Hadley Badminton Club in Barnet, one night on a Thursday, Mike picked teams of 2 boys versus 2 girls. I was keen to play against an international standard player like Gillian and thought that playing two boys against two girls would make it easy for us to win.

Mike must have guessed what I was thinking because he turned round to me and quipped, *'You'll never beat them you know.'*

I grinned at him and replied, *'You want a bet on it?'*

*'Sure, a fiver'*

And that was the bet. None of the other players or club members knew there was a bet on. My partner's sister was playing with Gillian, and she turned out to be the weakest player, so Gillian had to work harder to cover her shots as well. We won the game by a very close 1 or 2 points and when we came off the court, I held my hand out to Mike with a big grin on my face and said, *'You owe me a fiver Mike'*

Gillian heard us and asked *'what's that fiver for?'*

*'Because you lost'* I replied. *'Mike bet me that you would win.'*

*'Oh'* she said, with a stern look on her face, *'I was taking it easy on you all.'*

And with that fiver we all had drinks together in the bar. We've been good friends ever since. Mike Goodwin's daughter worked in my greengrocer's shop for a short time before going on to train to be an airline pilot

Gillian Gilks was simply an amazing, formidable person on and off the court. That game against her and my partner's sister was when I saw that she was a cool, calm player who had a very natural game. If I had a chance to play mixed doubles again,

Gillian Gilks would be my partner of choice. She has a lot of confidence which makes you raise your game. It's been really nice to have a friend like her both on and off the court. She's been very supportive of both my badminton and work efforts. She even came to do a photo shoot for publicity when I opened my own greengrocer's shop after I lost my leg. Gillian had a cottage in Totteridge and for around 5 years I looked after her garden. She organized the trip to Guernsey for the competition against the 3 County Teams. They had one international player as well, and this was my first ever experience of going abroad to play badminton. I went on to play lots of tournaments abroad even after I lost my leg.

I've learnt a lot through playing with good badminton players like Mike, Brian, Dick, Charlie and Gillian and watching them play too. I've learnt to be a very serious person who likes following the rules on court. I try not to cheat anyone but if someone cheats whilst playing against me, I will show them. I like winning a point fairly and squarely and I'm quite prepared to argue if necessary. Most people will say that I am a very nice person on court but if an opponent tries to intimidate me, I intimidate them back.

I was really fit before losing my leg. Afterwards, I tried a few different sports but still found that badminton was the best one to get me from A to B around the court. It was very good for fitness; you can eat quite a bit but you are burning and sweating it off on the court. It helped me because had I not been a badminton player before I lost my leg, my wounds would have taken longer to heal. The badminton winter season ran from September to April. In September 1980, I'd come out of hospital and been measured for my first limb, but I had not been for the first fitting yet. I was still using crutches everywhere I went. It was my birthday, and I was sitting in bed feeling really miserable and sorry for myself. I really missed playing badminton and the beginning of the season was always good fun. That's when I decided, *'Enough is enough.'*

I put my tracksuit on, put my kit bag over my shoulder and started heading towards the door. Kamalpreet Kaur looked at me angrily and asked, *'What do you think you are doing? Where on earth are you going dressed like that?'*

*'I'm going to badminton, to sit in the pub with everyone,'* I shouted back grumpily and slammed the front door loudly.

I hobbled off down the road, kit bag, crutches and no left leg and felt the adrenaline drive me forward. Then, about a mile down the road, it started to rain, and rain and rain. The crutches got more difficult to handle and the kit bag felt heavier and heavier. But I didn't care. I was determined I was going to get to the club and socialise with my friends. I needed their company, and I was fed up being in the house and not being able to do anything all day. I was absolutely drenched by the time I reached the club. They were all really angry with me and asked why I hadn't rung any of them to come and pick me up in the car instead of struggling along on crutches in the rain.

'I didn't decide until the last minute,' I replied defensively. I knew they were concerned for me, but I was determined not to be the victim. When I walked through the door, they already had 15 members there. Club rules state that if a 16th member comes then you must play a shorter game. Badminton games went to 15 points at that time, but now I was there it meant that games finished at 11 points. The other club members all groaned when I walked in. They wanted long games, but someone put my name on the board. I think they did it as a joke initially but then decided that they'd get me to play. So, some club members thought it was funny, those that wanted longer games didn't like it and some wanted me on the court for my encouragement.

And that was when I played my first match without a leg and won! I hadn't intended to play, just watch and enjoy everyone's company. My partner was Mike Mansell of the Flying Feathers. I played that game hopping around on one leg without the crutches. I fell so many times but got up each time and carried on playing.

It was such a good feeling to be back on court and winning that I just didn't care about falling or hurting myself or anything like that. Later on in the pub, as I joined everyone for a cold drink and banter, I felt a really sharp pain in my chest. We all thought it was because I'd been hopping around on one leg and fallen. Just a bit of a bruise and not used to using those muscles after so many weeks of not playing. That night it became more painful, so I ended up in hospital where they told me I had 2 broken ribs. There was nothing they could do apart from give me painkillers and tell me not to do anything exciting. Especially not laughing because that was when it really hurt! The badminton club members didn't know for a week what had happened as I didn't tell them until I got back to the club. I didn't actually play badminton for 3 months after that because I went to India. I knew then that nothing was going to stop me from playing badminton again. If I could do this well hopping around on one leg, imagine what I could do when I got my prosthetic!

At the end of May 1983, I got a letter from the Barnet District Badminton League inviting me to their annual general meeting. They wanted to present me with the Keith Holden trophy because of the successful efforts I had made playing badminton with a prosthetic leg. I'd only started playing properly again in 1981, a year after my amputation. It had taken two years of really hard work and I was the only disabled person amongst 90-plus clubs at that time.

When the letter arrived, Kamalpreet Kaur took a look at my face and asked, *'What's wrong?'*

I told her about the letter and my mixed emotions on receiving it. I was proud, happy, emotional but upset too.

*'Did they just give this to me because they feel sorry for me?'* I asked her, feeling that nagging pang of self-doubt and disbelief in my ability. She told me not to be silly and got the committee to explain things to me. There had been a good article in the local newspaper earlier that month mentioning me and the badminton club which had also impressed them.

*'You got nominated to receive the trophy because of your achievements. It's a committee decision and everyone was impressed by how well you were playing since your accident,'* they said when they came to the greengrocers to make sure I would be coming to the presentation. The trophy itself is a testament to the encouragement and support I received from everyone after losing my leg. I didn't have anyone come up to me and say that I couldn't play with them now I was disabled. Sure, I had to work as hard as everyone else did. Perhaps not having my left leg meant I had to work a bit harder to make sure I stayed at the same level as everyone else? But I could only have worked as hard as I did because of the encouragement I received from the badminton community whilst learning to live life with just one leg.

It meant a lot to me to receive the award. It said to me that my peers, colleagues and badminton players that I looked up to thought a lot about my efforts. It was a touching moment and a surprise to everyone. The only people who knew about it beforehand were the committee and me. On the day of the AGM there were about 40-50 people from all the clubs in the area in the room. Winning anything like that and being presented with it in front of so many people is like being given a huge dose of happiness. It was almost as good as winning a tournament! The Keith Holden trophy was one given by a well-known family of badminton players.

The trophy is a pair of solid silver candlesticks. Keith Holden was a member of Hadley Club from the late 70s onwards. His father, mother and brother used to play for St Mark's Badminton Club in the church hall, then their membership became smaller and smaller, so they amalgamated with Hadley. They were both Barnet clubs. We played against each other on club nights. He was much older than I was and at the time I had two legs. He was a very smart looking boy; a good badminton player, and the talent ran through the family. His brother came and played once or twice at Hadley, and I met his mum at a Christmas party but never saw her play. I only knew them from Hadley Club. He was on the committee of the Barnet District League and his parents decided they wanted to carry on the Holden name by running a competition and presenting a trophy. He retired from the club a couple of years after I lost my leg, but the trophy is still with me, and I look back on that time fondly.

After I won my first disability competition, I contacted local papers and asked them if they wanted the story. I wanted them to show the shop, the prosthetic leg and my badminton racquet in the photos they took. Eventually they would compete between themselves to get to the story first. This just grew and grew, and now I have a collection of cuttings about my badminton efforts from

» **Spanish papers**

» **German papers**

» **Indian papers/ Indian TV / Indian newspaper in Southall,**

» **Local London papers and**

» **Guernsey papers when I played as an able bodied player before losing my leg.**

Each time I won a competition I would get a write up in the local paper showing off the Yonex badminton racquet. Gillian Gilks suggested that the company might sponsor me. I wasn't sure about doing something like that but she brought me around and finally I sent a letter to them.

Yonex responded positively and I secured a contract of support for a badminton racquet. I was so pleased. It gave me a warm glow inside knowing that the company rated my competitive efforts highly enough to sponsor me. To compete to the best level that you possibly can, besides having the best fitting leg the next thing you need is the best racquet. And there were no better racquets at the time than those made by Yonex. They were professional, light and strong. Their sponsorship lasted about 12 years and might have continued longer if it hadn't been for our first international tournament in The Netherlands.

Things had been going so well up to that point. I was in the final against Colin Broadbridge, an ex-policeman, in a mixed doubles final. I was enjoying the match. Colin was doing a lot of clearing and trying to make me move around the court. I enjoyed playing mixed doubles even before I lost my leg. My favourite shots were the cross court drop shots. Aiming at the weaker player of a mixed doubles pair and picking the point off him or her. I was the only guy who was an amputee, all the others had both arms and legs. Some were born with shorter arms because of thalidomide; only Colin had a left arm in a sling because he had suffered a stroke.

He tried to smash the shot when his racquet broke.

'What's wrong, Colin?' I looked at the worried expression on his face as he searched frantically in his kit bag.

'My racquet's broken. Oh no, I don't believe it. I haven't got another one. Where on earth is it? I can't finish playing the rest of the match against you.' he replied hurriedly, trying very hard to keep his anger and frustration at the situation under control. I was in a bit of a predicament. If he couldn't play on, then my partner and I would be declared the winners. And he and his partner would be declared the runners up. And if I lent him my racquet we could carry on with the match. If I beat him, it would be done fair and square through my badminton efforts rather than by him conceding. I looked at the other two players who were chatting leisurely to each other on the court waiting for us to return and decided. 'No problem, Colin. Don't stress. Here, use my racquet. I've got another spare one in case I need it.'

'Are you sure, Meva?' he asked hesitantly because badminton players are as particular about their racquets as tennis players are about theirs and as cyclists are about their bikes or cricketers are about their bats. Our racquets are like gold to us. They are our lucky charms, our mascots, our winning formula tool and everything else besides. Lending your racquet to someone is like giving them the shirt off your back and shows how much you trust them. It's a real test of friendship.

So, we both went back onto the court to carry on playing and, just my luck, he and his partner beat us! He was so impressed with the racquet, and I was pleased for him. Only later was I informed by Yonex that they would no longer continue to sponsor me because lending my racquet to others was a breach of the terms of my contract. Well, if I'd only known that at the time! It really added insult to injury after losing the match.

I was kicking myself that I'd broken such a term of my contract. I couldn't literally kick myself obviously as it would have hurt big time with one metal leg, so I had to imagine it instead. Then I got angry as to why they should have such a silly rule like that anyway. Could they not see that it was an honest situation whereby a team-mate breaks their racquet, needs to continue playing and the quickest thing to do is ask to borrow another team-mate's racquet, especially if they didn't have any other spare racquets left in their bag? It all felt so unfair! That's why they tell everyone to read the small print nowadays. It makes a big difference and breaking that small rule just to help a team-mate cost me a lot of support from a major badminton racquet company. There was nothing I could do or say to them to change their minds on the decision to withdraw their support. It was so frustrating. I carried on playing without a sponsorship contract for a while until, eventually, I got one from Carlton to cover the cost of clothing and racquets.

Blatchford prosthetics manufacturers started sponsoring the sports legs I needed from late 1992 when carbon fibre sockets came in, so I made sure that the leg, racquet and clothing were in pictures in the papers after each tournament I played. It provided good publicity for them. I was competing a lot, and winning a lot, so the companies were willing to take the risk with me and back me in my efforts.

## ∾ Finally, Off Zero, But My Opponent's the Hero ∾

I always play to win but sometimes you come across players who outclass you in every way. That is when all you can do is try to score a point or two from them. Before I lost my leg and in my early badminton days, I lost in a singles match 15-0 to a club member. It felt so awful that I promised myself I never wanted to see a zero-point score again.

I've stuck fast to that rule ever since. It makes me fight hard to get that first point. One time, after losing my leg I ended up playing a really strong player named Dan Bethel, now seeded number 1 in the UK and, currently number 2 in the world. He has cerebral palsy and his classification meant we were placed to play against each other. Overall, those with cerebral palsy end up with severe weakness in their muscles but it's not the same as an amputee who has no leg there at all.

He was getting the upper hand all the time because I wasn't getting clearance. He is quite tall, and my big mistake was to let him serve even though I won the toss. As he was left-handed my forehand would naturally go to his backhand, but his height meant I couldn't get the clearance I needed to win a point against him. The only way I could get a point would be if I could force him to make an error during play.

He was making me move around the court a lot. Playing on half a court which is long and narrow is hard for amputees. And it's difficult to play against a determined youngster like Dan. A young, tall, slim, strong player – he's a beast! It was one of the toughest matches I have played in a long time against him.

I have known him for many years, since he was a youngster, and he has come on tremendously since those early days. I look forward to cheering him on in the 2021 Paralympic Games in the final!

My first game against him went so badly wrong. He totally thrashed me 21-0. I was dumbstruck. I never lose that badly. Ever! It was demoralising and made me lose confidence. I gave myself a severe talking to before the second game started but there it was again. Already he was 17-0 up. I hadn't even got 1 point off him. I was determined not to be on zero for two whole games so the next point I forced him to make an error and won it. Finally, I was off zero. I jumped up and punched my fist and racquet into the air in joy. He still won the match but after getting off zero I really didn't care how many points I got in that second game. The most important thing was to get that very first point and not lose with two zeros.

Having highly aspirational role models all around you makes it easier to do well in your own life and career. As a young child in India my role models were the people of my village and my grandfather. After partition in 1947 (India / Pakistan) the main village sports were hockey and mud wrestling. During the 1950's through to the 1970's there were no televisions, desktop or laptop computers, games consoles, or smartphones. There was only radio coverage available in the village.

On coming to England, I discovered football and started following it regularly. George Best, Bobby Charlton, Jackie Charlton, Bobby Moore, Geoff Hurst, Martin Peter and Alan Ball were my main heroes. The England football team had won the World Cup in 1966, so these players were regularly in the newspapers that I delivered.

My cousin Resham Singh Maan preferred watching cricket. I first saw cricket being played in 1968 in Delhi. When we were in Nanaji's restaurant together we would cheer on Bishan Singh Bedi, a left-arm bowler who played for India between 1966-1979, taking 266 wickets during his Test cricket career. I really liked Bedi because he was quite outspoken. If he didn't agree with something, he said so. And he always wore colourful turbans when he was competing.

When I am not playing badminton, I really enjoy running. I have run a few races against amputees in the weekend games events and I have also completed some fundraising marathons for different charities. My two role models in running are firstly Milkha Singh, who won the gold medal in the 400m sprint at the Asian and Commonwealth Games during the 1960's. He was nicknamed affectionately 'The Flying Sikh.' More recently, the marathon runner Baba Fauja Singh is my other running role model. He is one of the oldest to have run the London Marathon in 2003 with a time of 6 hours, 2 minutes, beating several record times in different age brackets.

The nearest I could get to mud wrestling on television in the UK was wrestling and boxing in a ring (without the mud!). My hero Muhammad Ali (Cassius Clay) was one of the best, his nickname was The Greatest. It is important to have political as well as sporting heroes in your life and for me this was Manmohan Singh, who served as the 13th Prime Minister of India (2004-2014). In the UK my role model for politics was Margaret Thatcher, whom I met whilst she was canvassing for votes in the elections.

Sports that Sikhs enjoy most are hockey, kabadi or cricket, so without other Sikh badminton role models I looked to an outstanding Indian player, Prakash Padukone for inspiration. I saw him in 1980 when he won the All England Open at Wembley Arena and the atmosphere during his final match was electric. In 1994, he set up India's first Badminton Training Academy and continues to coach and mentor upcoming badminton talent in the country these days through the Prakash Padukone Badminton Academy within the Padukone-Dravid Centre for Sports Excellence (CSE). The co-founder of the CSE is also a national and state level Indian badminton player, Vivek Kumar.

Staying with the themes of philanthropy and politics, one of my latest heroes must be Ram Singh Rana, Golden Hut Punjabi Dhaba for supporting the farmers' protests against the latest agricultural laws in Delhi, India. He saw that the farmers needed food and shelter and opened his bed and breakfast dwellings for them all free of charge since November 2020 to 13th December 2021. The Indian Government under Prime Minister Narendra Modi changed their stance on 19th October 2021 and all the farmers returned to their farms. I mention Ram Singh Rana here by way of a special thank you for all that he did to help the farmers of India.

The pinnacle of my sporting career must be 2016, the year I was nominated to be a Sikh Role Model. The Sikh Role Model (www.sikhrolemodel.org) is a conglomerate of Sikh icons all over the world who have outshone others with their excellent achievements in various fields. It is a platform to bring together the most prominent and influential Sikh personalities who are doing tremendously well in their lives. Sikh Role Models act as inspiration and guides for upcoming Sikh generations who may need mentors and teachers to set up their entrepreneurial footprints in a highly competitive world.

The nominations may be in any of 13 categories such as academia, medicine, politics, military, entrepreneur and arts as well as others. I was nominated within the sports category for all my efforts within badminton. It was an auspicious occasion collecting my award at an event in London. I am now portrayed alongside great Sikh sports people from the world of boxing, weightlifting, marathons and more. When you are nominated by your own cultural and religious community for the sport to which you have given most of your life, it is a humbling experience. It is an immense honour to receive it.

It was a total surprise to me when I was nominated. Sarabjeet Singh Sabharwal, a Sikh I knew through the Gurdwara had put in the nomination unknown to me. He showed me what he wrote in the application, and I found it so touching. It read:

*'I first met Meva Singh ji a few years ago on the day of the Gurdwara's general election. He inspired me to become a social welfare secretary and supported me fully. With the help of Meva Singh ji and other volunteers we were able to convert the Gurdwara's Langar Hall into a badminton court and opened it to both children and adults. Since then, Meva has committed himself to coach anyone who is interested in learning badminton. I invited Meva to the Punjabi School and Summer Camp where he inspired hundreds of children with the story of his journey. As I truly believe that Meva is a great role model and wonderful down to earth human being therefore I am forwarding his name to be published on the Sikh Role Model website. I would also like to invite him to speak at the Inspired Dinner Club evening event as a guest speaker. To share his incredible story with Sikh entrepreneurs.'*

It took the Sikh Role Model administrators around a year to fact check everything about me. I had my own website with all my badminton achievements on it so that helped to make it easier for them. The nomination for the Sikh Role Model came on top of the recognition for my badminton efforts that I received in 2011 by the United Khalsa Sports Academy (UKSA) and in 2013 by the British Sikh Council UK. I am now proudly profiled on the Sikh Role Model website in their Sports category. It makes me feel so humbled and honoured that all my badminton efforts are being recognised within the Sikh community throughout the UK and beyond alongside other great Sikh sports people.

Being a guest speaker at the Inspired Dinner Club evening was an amazing emotional experience. It took place on Wednesday 16th May 2018, at Flock Restaurant London EC3N 1LA. I went there by tube and was met at Aldgate Tube Station by Sarabjeet Singh Sabharwal. We walked the short distance to the restaurant. There were only 4 or 5 others in the room but within 20 minutes everyone was there. 35 to 40 people from all different walks of life seated around 8 tables. Charity workers, businessmen and many other fields and professions.

Jatinder Palaha, who is responsible for the IT functions within Sikh Role Model and Sukhi Wahiwala, Board Chairman of Sikh Role Model came and chatted whilst we were waiting for the other guests to arrive. I was wearing a tracksuit and my England T-shirt. I took shorts to change into for the speech so people could see my leg. I only knew one other person in the room, a man who comes to the Nanak Darbar North London Gurdwara. He recognised me and we chatted and caught up as I had not seen him in a while. As we were standing by the bar, a young lady came up to me and said: *'Hello Uncle ji, mum said to say hello if I saw you here. I told her you would be speaking at the event.'*

I was a bit flustered initially as I couldn't think who she was referring to but it soon came back to me. Her mum and dad were from the same village as my mum, Mehsampur; that's how we knew each other.

It was a private event so there were no other customers in the restaurant. The restaurant itself is under a railway arch. The food was very nice, and there were plenty of vegetarian options and soft drinks. When it was my turn to speak, I stood up by the bar with a microphone in my hand. I was a little nervous speaking, but everyone thoroughly enjoyed it. I told them some of the stories that I have included in this book, so they had a bit of a sneak preview of the many badminton adventures I want to share with the world. There was a video made of the speech, and I showed them the leg and told them how I really pushed myself hard to achieve and succeed. They even laughed at some of my jokes about prosthetics.

It was a fantastic evening. I am even more honoured to have been asked to be the official Ambassador of the Sikh Games (due to take place in 2023) by Mandeep Kaur Moore which, after all the lockdowns and restrictions over the past two years, I am really looking forward to putting my energy into.

# Chapter 5
# Keep It. You Need It More Than I Do.

Tears of joy came to my eyes as I read the advert in the Barnet and District Local Advertiser again for what seemed like the 100th time that day (according to my wife!), but it was probably only the 15th time. I still couldn't believe it was real and had to keep reminding myself by reading it repeatedly.

*'Churchill High Class Fruiterers, under new management, Meva Singh Dhesi, Grand Opening 29th April by Gillian Gilks.'*

We'd just had our Grand Opening! Kamalpreet Kaur and I had been working solidly around the clock getting ready for that day. The fruit and vegetables were all nicely laid out. Everything gleaming and spotless, all signs and prices arranged neatly. The newspaper reporter from the Barnet and District Local Advertiser had taken several photographs of Gillian Gilks with two of her Commonwealth badminton gold medals. We grinned solidly throughout the whole day and posed like seasoned professionals with a carefully prepared basket of fruit for the photographs that were going to be in the newspaper.

Closing the store after that first busy, exciting week; tired but very happy, I kept looking at the advert in a bit of a daze. I still couldn't believe the shop was ours and we had our own flat upstairs, so we were finally alone together. No more living with the parents. Absolute bliss! The condition being that Monday to Friday we had to wake up at 3.30am to open the shop by 7am and keep going until 6pm. On Fridays we opened until 7pm so people could pick up their groceries as they came home from work. We would deliver free locally for anyone spending more than £5. It was hard work making sure all our customers were satisfied, paying all the bills and invoices and filling in the business tax returns. But it meant I spent more time with my wife because we were working together which was the best bit. We were doing this for each other, and we enjoyed every minute of it.

After returning from India in March 1981 I was desperate to get back to work doing something I knew. I'd been medically retired from London Transport Buses following the accident because they didn't have automatic gearing on their buses. After losing the leg I was unable to keep driving for them or for the mini cab company where I had been moonlighting because officially I was still employed by London Transport. Initially I went for a job interview as a driver and the owner wouldn't give me the job because of my leg. I was really perplexed. What could I do to start earning a wage again to pay the bills and support my family? Driving a bus or taxi was the only thing I knew. And the only other job I knew anything about was the greengrocers.

When I came to the UK as a teenager I couldn't read, write or speak English. The only language I knew was Punjabi. I learnt English by reading the football results in the Sun because it was a small paper, so, easy to start with. I read other papers when I got a newspaper delivery round. Then I got a weekend job at the local greengrocers in Ballard's Lane, Finchley and speaking with the owners and customers helped me improve my language ability immensely.

The Lesters owned and ran the greengrocers. They were a hard-working Jewish family who lived in Wembley. There was Derek Lester, the husband; a bubbly, friendly, soft-spoken man who loved betting on horses. His father used to own the local betting shop. Derek had a lot of time for me, telling me the names of all the fruits and vegetables and showing me how to write the names and prices on the tickets. And there was his wife Val, their son John and Val's older sister Charlotte.

The Jewish community had come to London during the two World Wars and settled in many parts of the city. Finchley, Golders Green, Woodside Park, Market Place and East Finchley were the main Jewish community areas. There weren't that many Jewish families in Barnet. The Lester family were an example of the kind, caring family and community-oriented people I got to know fairly early on during my teenage years after coming to the UK. Derek Lester's family (in-laws) were wholesalers in Covent Garden and Spitalfields. He started out as a wholesaler in the market before opening his first greengrocer's shop in Finchley Central. He then opened and ran 3 more shops, North Finchley, East Finchley and High Road. The very last one he opened was in Market Place Wembley. I worked in all of them apart from the Wembley shop. He knew how to buy good quality fruit and vegetables at the right price because he had been a wholesaler.

Neither of the sisters could drive at the time so every Thursday, Friday and Saturday they would come in a taxi between 5.30am-5.45am to open the shop. I would pass the greengrocers whilst doing my newspaper round at 5.45am but I never took much notice of them. The newsagent's shop was in Ballards Lane, aptly named Ballard's News. Around two weeks after they first saw me, they asked if I would help them lift the old heavy wooden shutters; the type that you had to push manually. As a fit and strong 14-year-old I was happy to oblige and among the three of us we managed to heave the creaking shutters up to open the shop.

Not long after that they offered me a job boiling beetroot in a copper pot at the back of the shop. My job was to make sure there was enough water in the pot and light the stove, so it was cooking by the time Derek came in from the market in the morning. I used to get £1 a week for the paper round walking all the streets whatever the weather. They gave me ten bob (50p in today's money) for 2 weeks of boiling beetroot at the back of the shop out of the bad weather. Doing both jobs meant I earned some good pocket money to help my mum pay the household bills. I boiled beetroot in the early mornings for a week or two then they offered me a job after school. I didn't ask what they were going to pay me, but they offered me £2.50 working 5 days a week after school. I said I'd do it 3 days a week to start off with to see how it went.

I liked the older sister Charlotte better than Derek's wife, Val. She was friendlier. Val was shorter than me and I found her hard. She worked hard and was a hard person. I didn't like her that much. I always used to argue with her. I gave as good as I got and that was why she liked me. She could see that I was no pushover and wasn't standing for it. Derek Lester's son John was older than me. He went into the army to do national service in Israel. The older sister Charlotte (the nicer one) was taller than me. She had no children of her own, so I used to call her mum. There was always a lot of work to do when I was there with them, but they paid good money.

Val and Charlotte were both big smokers. Their favourite brands were Embassy Light and Benson and Hedges. Every Saturday they gave me a fiver to go to the shop to get 200 cigarettes for each of them. One week Val would pay, the other week Charlotte would pay. In those days, for a fiver you would get 400 cigarettes. They would keep packets of each brand in each of their houses so when they visited each other they did not have to remember to take their cigarettes with them. I still remember the way they would light up and inhale that first deep hit of nicotine smoke and tar. Their faces used to change right in front of me, almost as if they were in a trance-like state. Like a drug, like cocaine, or hashish or something. But it still didn't tempt me to try. It stank!

Although both sisters smoked heavily, Derek and John didn't smoke at all. Their brothers didn't smoke either. Charlotte and Val would smoke more at home than at work. They did not smoke in the shop, only in the back room. The smell of the smoke was yuck! Charlotte would always hug me as a greeting, and I could smell the cigarette smoke on her. It made me grimace which made her laugh. She used to look after me a lot. I was still at school and working during weekends. After I left school, I went to work for my cousin in his restaurant for a year and then went back to work full time for them.

Val, Charlotte and Derek taught me from a young age to know when people are respecting you and when they are insulting you. When I worked weekends for them as a youngster, I used to do deliveries of fruit and vegetables in boxes. I had to box up the groceries and walk to local houses to deliver them. Sometimes, the customer's house was a long walk from the shop. One lady lived around half a mile away and I used to walk there with a heavy, awkward box on my shoulder. I'd always try to make it as much fun as possible whilst I went to take my mind off how heavy the box was. First it was Finchley Main Road, then left into Lover's Walk. Next, I'd go over the bridge, stopping quickly to catch my breath whilst trying to guess which trains were running on the northern line underneath and imagine that someone I knew was on that train. Inwardly, I wished them well as they sped on their way. Finally, I'd head down the hill and hit the main road. The house was a few hundred yards further down Finchley Way. She spent around £4-5 per week so she was a good customer.

When I delivered her box, she gave me 2 pennies as a tip. Back at the greengrocer's shop I held out the coins angrily in front of the sisters and said, *'Look, she gave me 2 pennies! I walked all the way from the shop to her door and all she gave me was 2 pennies.'*

Those coins felt like they were burning a hole in my palms. I was that angry. They told me that next time if she gives me the same then I must say to her: *'You keep it, you need it more than I do.'*

So that was what I did! The following week, when I went to her house with her delivery she gave me sixpence, the old sixpence, which was 2 and a half new pennies. I did exactly as they told me. I said:

*'Sorry I am not taking this.'*

*'Why?'*

And with a sharp intake of breath, I blurted out quickly, *'Cos you need it more than I do.'* And ran all the way back to the shop as fast as my legs would carry me whilst she looked at my vanishing back in concerned bemusement!

*'How can she do that? Does she think I'm a slave or something? It's insulting to give such a small tip. She should be embarrassed. Better not to give anything at all than give too little,'*

I stammered out breathlessly when I got back to the shop, bent over, clutching my sides and trying to stop my lungs from hurting after all that running. I wouldn't have cared but I had my ordinary school shoes on, not my badminton trainers, so they really pinched my toes and hurt my heels as I ran in them. It wasn't that I didn't want the tip. It was the fact that it was such a small tip as to be insulting. Of course, she came storming into the shop later complaining that I'd been very rude. Luckily for me, the boss's wife, Val, already knew about it so she was well prepared to receive her and to sort the matter out.

When I got married, I couldn't get much of a pay rise, only one of £5, and now I had a wife to look after. It was 1978 and I was earning £85 per week for 6 days with very long hours. So, I left Derek, Val and Charlotte and went to work on the buses for 40 hours per week where the pay was better. I started out as a conductor and then went on to be a driver. I did the bus conductor's job for around 3 months on probation. My first trial at being a bus driver wasn't successful, they said that my arm was too short, so I continued being a conductor. It was in the days when there was a driver in a cab in the front of the bus and a conductor in the bus. The passengers got on at the back of the bus; there was no door in those days. The staircase to the next level was also at the back of the vehicle and the driver only left each bus stop when the conductor rang the bell.

As a bus conductor I had a ticket machine which hung at the front of my uniform by a strap around my neck. I had to roll the lever to generate a paper ticket for the passenger and I had a leather bag for the change. We used to pick up so many different people on our routes. One day, at the Hampstead Heath stop, Michael Foot got on the bus wanting to go to Whitehall. Politicians didn't have to pay for tickets, they were issued with a Gold badge which he showed me as he boarded. I didn't know who he was at the time, it was only when the bus driver told me that I realised.

I had another attempt at being a bus driver once I had been with London Transport for 6 months. We had a forward-thinking management at Chalk Farm Garage Harmood Street London NW1 which was our bus depot. Chalk Farm Garage was the first to employ a lady driver and a transgender driver. It is no longer there after being in operation for 70 years. It closed in 1993 and the site where it stood now has a block of flats built on it.

We had to learn 5 bus routes, 1 route each day. I would sit on a bus which was doing the route that day with my instructor who would talk me through specific points whilst the regular driver did the route. One day, we were on the Number 3 bus and had just reached Lambeth Bridge bus stop, which was the stop after Parliament House when we came to a total halt. The driver had switched the engine off, and the passengers were all asked to disembark. The bus had broken down! Another bus came along some minutes later and took the passengers on their journeys but as staff members we had to stay on board until the mechanic arrived. We made a good team, there were two West Indians (driver and conductor), myself and my instructor.

The mechanic took our bus to Victoria Garage. It was going to take at least an hour to get it fixed so we were given tea/coffee and biscuits whilst we waited. Once the bus had been fixed, we got back on the same route and picked up/dropped off passengers all the way to Crystal Palace. Not long after I started doing the bus driver's role, it was decided that a driver could also do the bus conductor's job if they changed the door from the back of the bus to the front.

I was enjoying my time as a bus driver in London. My grandfather on my father's side, Kartar Singh Dhesi, owned his own bus company in Dhesian Kahna in 1942 and was well known there. I felt proud to be doing something that he would commend me for. No sooner had I started settling in to being a bus driver, the strikes started. Typical, just my luck! This was 1978/79 and the 'winter of discontent' where public and private sector workers throughout the country went on official and unofficial strikes to protest the Labour Prime Minister, Jim Callaghan, and his government's policies. I had to join the strike when my bus company declared that they were going to support it. Unfortunately, when you go on strike you don't get paid, so I ended up getting a job as a minicab driver whilst this was all going on. You must make ends meet and be able to pay the bills no matter what is going on around you.

In all, I had been with London Transport for three and a half years by the time of my accident and was medically retired 12 months later. They gave me a 10-year pension payment which really helped during my recovery time. When the Lesters heard I was getting frustrated at not being at work after my accident, they gave me a job at their greengrocers just to get me out of the house. I worked for 3 days a week as a cashier. They did that even though I had been working for London Transport instead of them. That was how kind-hearted they were. They said:

*'All you have to do is just sit at the till and take the money.'*

By now, it was July 1981. My first child, a daughter, was born and I was happy with life. We named her Sarah Jane Kaur Dhesi to make it sound more English, so it would be easy for everyone to pronounce in school. She kept the name from birth until she was 18 years old. We felt it was then the right time to change her name to Kirendeep Kaur Dhesi as it was more in keeping with our Sikh culture.

I'd been working for around 6 months as a cashier for the Lester's and felt ready to take on more responsibility. I mentioned that I would like to run my own business and Derek Lester said I should look for a greengrocer near a fish shop and a butcher's shop. That way, I would get the customers who were passing by deciding they wanted to buy something there too.

Around the same time, my sister-in-law told me about an opportunity to do exactly that within the greengrocer's department of the Japanese Centre on Regent's Park Road, Finchley Central. It was the only one of its kind and we used to get Japanese people coming to shop there from all over the place, especially visitors to London from Japan. 95% of the customers were Japanese. It is now operating as an estate agent. My sister-in-law, Rushpal Kaur, told me the previous manager had just left the Japanese grocery and greengrocery business and was investing in property instead, and perhaps I might like to see if I could take on the greengrocery side of the business. So, I rented the floor space and looked after the whole greengrocery side, specialising in Japanese produce. I really enjoyed it and I was doing well developing a good customer base.

The greengrocer's section was directly at the front entrance. It was designed so that customers had to pay me for the produce first before they could carry on into the rest of the store. I saw more £20 notes in those days than I had ever seen before. Everyone paid in cash, so I always had to keep £10 and £5 notes handy for their change. One Saturday afternoon I had over £600 in my pocket. I didn't use a till or keep it in my wallet, I just had it in a paper bag that day. It was the amount of money that I needed to pay the shop rent. It was in my back pocket, and I used the bag to put my takings in from the day as well. It was a busy day being a weekend and nearer closing time I reached for it because I wanted to pay the manager the rent.

It wasn't there! I looked everywhere and I racked my brain trying to retrace my steps from the last time I remembered putting some takings in there. Nothing. It was gone. £600 plus a bit extra! Gone! As I was sweating and panicking about it, the manager of the centre came over and asked me what was wrong. I told him I had lost his rent for that month.

*'Why didn't you give it to me first thing this morning? I could have locked it up in the safe for you. What does it look like? How much is in it?'* he asked.

I told him, *'It's a plain brown bag with mainly £20 notes in it. There was at least £600 but also my takings and the change from my purchases of stock at Covent Garden, but I don't know exactly how much that was.'*

*'Should I call the police? Did you think that one of the customers might have picked it up and not handed it in? A report will need to be made of the incident as it was a fair amount of money, so perhaps we should go to my office to do this,'* he responded gently.

*'I don't think the police will be able to do anything about it,'* I replied as we walked to his office. *'It's my own silly fault, I can't blame anyone but myself for mislaying it in the first place.'* When we reached his office he looked at me seriously and said, *'Yes, I expect that might be what you think about this now. It's natural to feel like that. How would you feel if someone had found it? What would you give to get that money back?'*

I was worried and upset so even though I thought it such an odd, cryptic question for him to ask I replied in desperation:

*'Anything, I'd give anything the person wants if the money is found!'*

With that he went out of the door and came back with a young Indian boy beside him. I was becoming even more confused by then, wondering how on earth I would be able to pay the shop rent and whether they would charge me interest because of late payment. What on earth would Kamalpreet Kaur have to say when I told her I had lost over £600? That was the worst thought ever, and I held my head in my hands, looked down at the floor and tried to control the panic building up inside me. All these thoughts were buzzing wildly through my head, so I didn't even notice that the manager had gone to the safe and given the young lad a brown bag.

The manager said to me, *'How much did you say was in the bag?'*

*'Oh,'* I groaned, shaking my head in my hands still looking dejectedly at the floor, *'over £600 but I don't know the exact amount because I didn't count what I was adding to it throughout the day.'*

I was so distraught I didn't even recognise the bag that the young lad now had in his hand. I was focusing on how irresponsible my answers must have sounded to the centre manager. It was so important to know exactly how much money you took and how much you spent. It is a basic rule, and one which I now found myself unable to answer. Just listening to myself saying that made me feel even worse inside. My wife was not going to be happy with me when I got home. I could just feel it. It had been a long, busy day and it just seemed to be going from bad to worse, whilst I was in the office with the manager and this young lad.

*'So if someone found it, you'd give them anything they asked for, is that correct?'* the manager asked me again while looking directly at the young man.

*'Yes,'* I replied, feeling even more confused as to why the young man was there with us that evening. *'Anything. But I don't see how it can be found.'*

So, the manager asked the young man to tell us what he could about the brown bag he had in his hands.

*'It was lunchtime boss, and I was in the kitchen. I just entered as Meva left with a cup of tea. I found this bag on the floor, behind the kitchen counter. I saw it had a lot of money in it, so I brought it over to you and you put it in the safe.'*

I stared open-mouthed at the young man. Relief and gratitude flooded over me in a huge tidal wave. Yes, I had gone quickly over to the staff kitchen to make myself a cup of tea which I took back to the shop. I remembered now. It was too busy with customers to stop for a full lunch break. The bag must have dropped out of my back pocket when I bent over to get the milk from the small fridge in the kitchen, brushing against the edge of the kitchen counter as I did so, and I didn't notice it fall out. There were no coins in it that would make a noise if they landed on the floor, only notes.

I was so overcome by his honesty and integrity that day in handing that brown bag over to the manager. I asked him what I could give him to say thank you for finding it. I offered him some money, but he replied,

*'No thank you. I am just glad I could be of help. If I had wanted money, I would have kept the lot and not handed it in'*

He laughed good-naturedly as he said it, and with a nod of his head to us he turned to leave the room. There was £790 in that brown bag that day. I paid the manager the rent with relief, thanked the young man again as he walked out of the office and made my way home to my wife and family; grateful that I didn't have to tell her that I had been unable to pay the rent. There are some conversations that you seriously don't want to have in your married life, and this I can safely say, would have been one of them.

After around six months at the Japanese Centre, I decided I'd like to branch out, buy my own shop premises and do it for real. They had put the rent up on the floor space three times in those six months at the Japan Centre, so I felt it was the right time to move on. That's when we heard that the owner of a greengrocery shop in Church Hill Road was selling up. One of my badminton associates, Phyllis Smith, first told me about it. She was better known in the badminton club as Phyl. Her husband, Les Smith, was the estate agent, trading under the name of Charles Law. They were both much older than I, and Les Smith was a steam engine fanatic, so they used to go to Yorkshire regularly. They would encourage me to buy a house rather than a car, but my father insisted on us living as a joint family in one house when I first got married and especially after my accident.

I looked at greengrocers shops in a few different areas before Phyllis told me about the Church Hill Road shop. I would drive around, go into any greengrocer shops that I came across, buy a bit of fruit or veg and start chatting to the owner about whether it was for sale or not. I heard that Phyllis passed away in 2020, but because of the Covid-19 restrictions on numbers of people allowed to attend funerals, I couldn't go along to pay my respects on the day. I went over to her house and chatted to her son when the restrictions had eased.

The Church Hill Road shop was at the top of the road just opposite the Kentucky Fried Chicken and a little further down was Oak Hill Park. Next door was a very nice butcher's shop. Bill Monday, a tall, grey haired, very English guy owned it, but I used to call him Tom. There was a small junior school just before Oak Hill Park. Mothers would come in after dropping their children off, so we developed a good relationship with them.

The greengrocers was a well-established business with regular customers and good staff. I was only the 3rd owner in 43 years. Nobody could believe that it was just two years since losing my leg. They were concerned I was taking on a lot of responsibility too early. But for me it was important to feel I was doing something that would support my wife and our family, and being a greengrocer was a job I knew. I went over there to buy something and just started chatting generally to the owner, Douglas Goodyear, who ran the business with his wife and father-in-law. He was quite friendly. When I mentioned I had been viewing shops he rolled his eyes and groaned:

*'If only I'd known. I've just taken this one off the market.'*

I must have looked quite crestfallen at that because he looked at me and said, 'Look, come into the back room here and let's chat a bit more.'

Over a cup of tea, he asked me why I wanted to run my own greengrocery business and we talked about it all thoroughly. At the end of that conversation, he sold the shop to me. Initially I was only going to buy it leasehold but because Douglas Goodyear had no children he said, 'Look, why don't you borrow money from the bank so you can have it freehold?'

Freehold is better than leasehold, so I was quite taken with the idea. At the time it looked like I was taking on a lot of risk. It was hard to get a loan from the bank because interest rates were extremely high, at around 16%. I tried my bank, Lloyds, but they wouldn't lend me the money. On my solicitor's advice I went to Barclays to ask them; my solicitor put in a good word for me, and I managed to get a 50% loan.

So, all I had to do was to find the other 50%. I had to borrow this from my family and arranged to pay it all back to them within one year. For a whole year I only had a wage of £25 per week to spend on housekeeping for my wife, my daughter and I to live off. Somehow, we managed and were happy. My mum gave us a table for the living room. And Kamalpreet Kaur even saved enough money to buy us a small television and three chairs to sit around the table. The only difficulty arose because Douglas Goodyear had dismissed the estate agent, Charles Law, just before we had our chat in the backroom. It meant Les Smith didn't get the commission for the sale. It was quite awkward at the badminton club for a while, but we eventually sorted it out. It was a tough lesson learnt. Never deprive your friends of income. Even if it's not your decision.

I was over the moon and really excited at being able to run my own business and be my own boss, setting the rules of the game for myself, keen to make my mark on this new venture. The shop was named after the owner, Douglas Goodyear. To make it clear that it was under new ownership, Douglas and I sat in the back of the shop one day and chatted about possible names over a cup of tea together.

*'Singh's greengrocers?'*

*'Dhesi fruit and vegetables?'*

None of those struck a chord with either of us, and we weren't certain that the regular customers would find those shop names exciting either.

*'What road are we on?'* I asked.

*'This road is called Church Hill Road and there is a park just down there called Oak Hill.'*

*'Hmm, so what if we called it Churchill, like the name of the politician? It's a popular name that people would recognise and remember easily.'*

He thought that was a good idea and got his sign printers to make the sign up for me. He was quite helpful during the whole process of selling the shop. As we sat there, he gave me lots of useful advice about his customers and their particular requirements. Mind you, I soon found out that running a greengrocers shop was a lot more demanding than playing a few games of badminton. Once we'd got full ownership of the premises, we put up the new sign, and kept the same shelving but changed the way the fruit and vegetables were laid out. We put a bigger display out on the pavement to attract passers-by. I opened a full 6 days a week in winter and extended that to 6 and a half days in summer.

To get the best fruit and vegetables for my customers I'd go to Covent Garden Market in the early morning 5 days a week. In the summer I'd also go to Spitalfields for their Saturday market. Every Tuesday and Friday the farmers used to deliver fresh vegetables such as potatoes, cabbages and rhubarb that they had grown locally in Bedfordshire. The farmers themselves would come and do the deliveries so it was always a good way to catch up on the news. How was the harvest? Children doing well at school? Any other issues they felt we should know about to keep our customers well supplied?

The local newspapers were excellent at printing stories and adverts for the shop for weeks after the opening. With their help throughout my time as the owner of Churchill's, word soon got around about the one-legged guy who ran a greengrocers shop and wanted to take part in the Paralympics playing badminton for England.

Well, you gotta dream ain't ye? And if you're going to dream, then DREAM BIG. That's what they always told me, anyway.

We were doing well, so two and a half years later, I bought my house in Totteridge as well as running the shop. It was 1984 and the interest rate on the house mortgage was now 19%! The banks were charging 16% plus an extra 3% just to arrange a loan with them. We made sure by then that we were on very good terms with the bank manager. We'd give the bank manager, postman, dustman, doctor and dentist Christmas cards and small presents each year. It was how it was done in those days.

Local celebrities would often come shopping in Church Hill Road. I got Bernie Winter's autograph one day. He and his brother Mike were well known BBC comedians. Bernie would come into the shop and ask for a carrier bag. They were not free at that time. If a customer spent around £5 then we might give them a free paper bag. Anyone who spent less, we'd charge 5p per bag. So, when he came in, I gave him a bag free a couple of times and asked for his autograph in return. He had an Old English sheepdog (the type you see in the Dulux paint adverts). After he'd been in a couple of times, I found out he used to get a carrier bag from me then go to the butchers next door and ask them for some free dog bones. He didn't buy anything from me or the butchers so after that, I started charging him 5p for the bag.

Plastic bag use had only just started and wasn't widespread, so we used paper bags. Most customers brought their own bags. For those that didn't have bags we would make cones out of newspaper and put the fruit and vegetables into those. Cone making out of newspaper was itself an art. First, we'd get a full sheet of newspaper, tear it in half and then place it on a hook. Then, as we needed them, we'd grab one sheet, fold it and roll it into a cone shape so the bottom of it was fully closed and nothing could fall out. Once the fruit or vegetables were in the cone, we'd fold up the top, so it was all easy to carry home. We'd use old newspapers as they were free and there were lots of them easily available. Our customers would give us their newspapers once they had read them. Carrots, onions, potatoes, cabbages were all wrapped like that. Brown bags were used for fruit. White paper was expensive, so only items like salad and beetroot went in white paper.

There were four other small greengrocery shops in our village so competition was quite tough, but we all talked to each other and helped each other out. There wasn't a big Sainsbury's in New Barnet. It opened 3 years after I bought my shop. Then the Sainsbury's in North Finchley opened as well. Local buses would go in the direction of the bigger stores and take customers away from the high street. That really affected our ability to continue the business. Around the time we sold up, I had four or five staff working for me. I had to pay their wages whether we had any customers or not.

Sometimes I'd be in work from 7am to 6pm lifting heavy sacks of potatoes, onions etc., then I'd come home, eat quickly and head straight out to the badminton club from 7-7.30pm until 11pm. The leg was starting to hurt too much with all of this, so we sadly made the decision to sell up. We sold it to a hairdresser, and it's changed ownership a few times since then. The last time I looked it was operating as a Suntan Salon and Massage Parlour.

## ∽ Meeting Celebrities and Royalty ∽

'Thank you for confirming that you will be attending the formal opening of the Douglas Bader Centre by HRH The Princess of Wales on Thursday 25th February 1993. Please find enclosed your formal invitation to the ceremony....'

*Signed by Air Marshall Sir Denis Crowley-Milling KCB CBE DSO DFC AE*
*Patron HRH Princess of Wales*
*President Lady Bader*

I remember it all as if it were yesterday. I'd just walked through into the kitchen and Kamalpreet Kaur said to me: *'Post's arrived.'*

There on the table was the envelope with the invitation letter, ticket, map and directions. I remember it so well because usually I only get handed the official brown or white envelopes that contain reminders for subscriptions, bills and charity donation requests. With the odd Sikh wedding invitation thrown in for good luck. Though my wife usually opens those and any other personal cards or letters that we get. She told me at the start of our marriage that was the best way to divide the post and we've stuck to it ever since. Though I do get to open my own birthday cards. We did compromise on that!

Wow! An invitation to attend the opening ceremony of the Douglas Bader Foundation Sports Centre at Queen Mary's Hospital in Roehampton. To see Princess Diana officially declaring the centre open. I was over the moon. If someone had asked me which was better, winning a badminton tournament or being in the same room as Princess Diana it would have been a tough question to answer. I mean, both situations give you the best feeling in the world, don't they? That sense of achievement and accomplishment when you win a tournament through sheer wits, determination and physical effort. And being invited to be in the same room as one of the best members of the Royal Family and perhaps even talk to her? What would I say? Would I be able to speak, or would I freeze if she asked me a question? Thoughts and emotions started swirling and flooding through my mind. I stood there grinning from ear to ear whilst Kamalpreet Kaur carried on bustling around me, oblivious to the contents of that envelope.

No matter how often I read it, it was still exciting. I couldn't contain the news. I was on top of the world and flying high inside. I told everyone. My children didn't believe me at first because I would often wind them up with tall tales of high achieving sports people, celebrities and royalty as a way of deflecting their concerns about my disability and to try to inspire them to achieve more in life for themselves. In fact, it became quite a bit of entertainment in our household as it was almost a case of:

'Wow, who's dad going to meet next?'

And children being children promptly switched off and went back to the things that were important to them like:

'Can you write me a note, so I don't have to do my homework?'

'Don't forget to buy me those new trainers today. You promised you would.' 'My best friend is having a party for her birthday, I'm going, aren't I?'

(Child speak roughly translates into 'you are going to drop me off and pick me up aren't you?') *'Do we have to go to Auntyji's place tomorrow? I'd really like to watch TV and you won't let me do that over there.'*

*'I'm not talking to my cousin because he said something horrible about me in school yesterday. Dad, will you tell him off for me?'*

And that was in the first five minutes before they had even had breakfast and if they didn't hurry up, they would be late for school. So, there was absolutely no way that I could let anything go to my head when there was all that to deal with, could I? I did get:

*'Well done. What on earth are you going to wear?'* from Kamalpreet Kaur which meant that she was really impressed and felt my excitement too. But the children soon took up all our time and attention again, so I didn't think much about it until they had gone to bed.

I'd been invited to the opening ceremony because the year before, I became badminton singles champion in the British Amputee Sports Day that had been held in Swindon, (1992). Richard Wilson, the actor who played 'Victor Meldrew' in the BBC sitcom 'One Foot in the Grave' presented me with my badminton singles winning medal that day. The previous winner had to give the Cup back to the organisers, and then they had to engrave my name on it, so it all took a while before I received that. But the medal was there for everyone to see. I showed it off to anyone who was interested, and to a lot more people who probably weren't, but I didn't care. I was proud of my achievement that day, and I wanted the world to know.

I had no idea who Richard Wilson was of course, even though he was right there in front of me presenting the medal. With a busy family life and an even busier badminton life the television doesn't really play much part for me. He had come especially from South Africa that morning, where he was shooting a film in Cape Town, just for the presentation. It took some doing for him to work out how to put the medal over my pink turban, and we made a bit of a joke about that. Luckily, it was my smaller one, otherwise it would have been really embarrassing for him. It was a proud moment, and I've got a framed photo of that presentation day in my living room which brings back so many good memories.

My leg at that time was still the all metal Mappe leg with a belt and hinges to keep it in place. There was one belt around the waist and one across the shoulder. I felt safe knowing I would not fall with those belts on. I had mine covered with soft foam so that aesthetically, when you wore trousers, it filled out to look like a normal leg. That was before the introduction of carbon fibre legs as sports legs and the trend to wear the metal uncovered came about. That leg broke the record for the 400m sprint at amputee sporting events twice, so it was a very good leg.

Thursday 25th February, the day of the opening ceremony at Roehampton was a cold, dry day. I looked across at the white badminton kit and white turban all laid out neatly in front of me and felt that tingling feeling of nervous excitement that you get when you know you are part of something big and historic. I had to be at Queen Mary's Hospital by 9.50am. The whole day was planned to run like a smooth operation.

Princess Diana was expected to arrive at 10am and would be met by dignitaries such as the mayor, government ministers and the trustees of the Douglas Bader Foundation. There was to be an amputee football team playing a demonstration match. She would also meet ordinary patients; the men, women and child amputees who would benefit from the facilities and services of the Centre.

Then she would officially open the Sports Hall by unveiling a commemorative plaque, sign the visitors' book and leave by around 11am. After she left, we would have some tea and sandwiches and take a good look around the sports facilities, trying things out if we wanted to. I felt quite smart with my badminton whites and brand new Endolite IP sports leg. This was one of my very first sports legs. It is the best of all the ones I've had over the years, and I've had many. More than I care to count. The new ones are more technologically advanced and different, but I still prefer my earlier ones.

I drove up and parked in the disabled bay near the hospital. I got there early so I had time to look around and freshen myself up before the ceremony. It was all very exciting. The traffic had been heavy on the way, so I had felt a little worried I might not make it in time. It took over an hour and a half for the journey. I had to use an A-Z map to find my way there as in-car satellite navigation systems were still being developed. Being a bus and mini cab driver really helped me find my way around London.

After I had freshened up, I was directed upstairs to the gym. There was a real buzz of expectation everywhere. I was asked to sit on one of the machines and demonstrate it when Princess Diana came. We stood around chatting with each other until we got the signal to get into our places. Princess Diana came in and the whole room looked in awe and admiration at her. She was dressed exquisitely in a beautiful green knee length dress. The room lit up as she walked along greeting the dignitaries and then went around chatting to some of us who were using the machines.

As she came to my machine, I felt my pulse starting to race in excitement. I was nervous and hoped she wouldn't notice the beads of sweat slowly gathering at the edges of my new white turban. I tried hard to control my breathing and speak clearly. We shook hands and I noticed she wasn't wearing gloves. She asked me who I was, what I was doing and why I was dressed in badminton whites. I chatted to her for a few short minutes about my badminton achievements and my family. She had such a nice manner. It was a great privilege, an absolute honour to have met her and spoken to her.

She laughed politely when I asked for her autograph and explained that Royal Protocol meant she wasn't allowed to give it to me. She performed the opening ceremony as the patron of the new Douglas Bader Sports Centre. That day I also met Mrs Bader, the wife of Sir Douglas Bader, a double amputee. The Douglas Bader Foundation was set up by family and friends of Sir Douglas Bader. It is a charitable organisation which supports amputees of all ages with an emphasis on those who have lost limbs as a result of aviation accidents / incidents. I'll never forget that day. I didn't manage to get into the official press photograph though. Somehow, they missed me out of the picture and there were no mobile telephones with cameras with which to take a selfie with Princess Diana like you would be able to do nowadays.

So, I've no other mementos apart from that invitation letter. The original hospital site, opened in 1915, was knocked down and rebuilt as a housing development. The plaque that Princess Diana unveiled is now proudly displayed at the sports centre in the new Queen Mary's Hospital site which opened in February 2006, and I see it every time I go there. The original opening day is one I will always cherish though.

## By Lyndon Williams

As Director of Welsh Badminton, I had been very positive about hosting the IBAD (International Badminton Association for the Disabled) World Championships in Cardiff in 2003 and using it to stimulate more disability development of badminton within Wales. As it was a World Championship and having no knowledge or information on what level we should pitch the delivery and presentation of the event, we decided to give it everything, bells, whistles and the rest, as we thought that Disability Badminton would, and should, expect nothing less.

Following on from the success of Cardiff, the Welsh Badminton Union and the Welsh team were thoroughly looking forward to our trip to Holland in The Netherlands for the Europeans and learning more about how disability events were run. Our trip to Holland would prove us very wrong. With 8 wheelchair athletes going to the Europeans and several standing athletes, plus support staff, we decided to minimise stress by hiring a large bus with wheelchair access and going by Ferry from Dover. Once this got out to the 'Disability' public we had several requests to 'give us a lift!!!'

However, space was at a premium and we were only able to offer the one and only English amputee, Meva, a lift and arranged to pick him up enroute at the Reading Services on the M4 motorway. Now, we were a little dubious as we were not sure Meva's organisational skills were quite in line with ours, however we set off with a pickup time and the service station agreed.

It was only when we were on the way that Meva rang and started to request changes to the pickup time and location; at one point asking us to go several miles UP the M25 as it was just as quick as going south on the M25 to DOVER!!!! The phone calls continued for some time, inevitably ending up back at Reading Services, the original collection point but quite a bit later time wise. On entering the bus, you can imagine the 'abuse' Meva received from the Welsh!!! (And well deserved, may I say.)

With minutes to spare we made it to the ferry and were on our way. The whole trip was a real experience. Hotel first and guess what? No disabled rooms! Not one of our players could get into their bathrooms so doors had to be taken off.

And that was just the start! I guess when things like this happen you work with the hotel and together, we made it work for everyone, but it was a little strained for a while.

Arriving at the hall? Again, there was absolutely nothing! At this point I started taking notes. We had to check we were at the correct place as there were no signs, or indication of a major European disability event soon to take place. In fact, there were no nets or posts up either! It was then we realised that our presentation of the Worlds 2003 was way beyond what had been the norm (we even had dry ice for the finals presentation) and that the organisation was very ad hoc.

I can safely say that is not the case anymore when it comes to Holland / The Netherlands staging any disability event. They are excellent, but back then, and not just Holland, disability maybe didn't have the profile and attention to detail it required. Thankfully after this we were able to get more involved and work with IBAD to set some standards that would move the sport forward. Players started to expect more and rightly so, and I think this was a small turning point in the making of disability badminton into the Paralympic sport it is today.

## ∾ The Long (and Sometimes Tortuous) Pathway From the ∾ Formation of IBAD to Becoming a Paralympic sport

By Lyndon Williams

IBAD or the International Badminton Association for the Disabled was formed in 1995. Exact details of who, why and when are sketchy however, Jim Frere (President), Jim Mackay and Ton Velberg were early founders to my knowledge. My first involvement with disability badminton came with an invite from Badminton England's Ian Wright (development) and Jake Downey (Head Coach) who had started working with a group of wheelchair players at a centre local to Milton Keynes. By that time Jake and Derek Batchelor had already delivered Badminton England's first Leaders' Award (Disabilities) in Bedford, which proved popular with both participants and carers.

I remember my session with Ian and Jake very well, as, whilst trying out a sports wheelchair for the first time, I managed to rip my thumb nail off! Still, other than that painful experience, seeing how badminton can be adapted for people in a wheelchair was a real eye opener and a challenge for me to go back to Wales and see if there was an appetite for this area of development. During the following period, IBAD staged several World Championships, first in The Netherlands 1998 followed by Germany 2000, and then Spain in 2001.

After the 2001 World Championships I was approached by Dr Jim Mackay, who I knew due to him now living in Wales (we all know each other in Wales!!) and asked if Welsh Badminton were interested in staging the 2003 IBAD World Championships. Well, we had no players and no disability plan, so why not, sounded like a great idea!!! Seriously, there was now a change across sport in general, and significantly so in Wales where creating opportunities for disabled people had become more of a focus, and I felt this was a great opportunity to kick start Welsh Badminton's disability plan. Now, where to find some players??? With help from Disability Sport Wales, we found some wheelchair players, who I immediately gave to our National Coach, Chris Rees and said,

*"There you go, six months to get them ready for the Worlds!"*

We approached the set-up of the Worlds as we would any other major event, gained UK sport funding, sponsors etc. and worked tirelessly to deliver what I believe was a great event and one I also believe started to change IBAD and disability badminton.

It was clear after this event that for IBAD to develop further it needed more support, greater interest across the globe and a solid development plan. I started to work more closely with IBAD and having looked back at various minutes from the meetings I could see that there was an obvious desire, but what was missing was the ability to sufficiently raise the profile and gain support on a global scale. We had very little clout. Yes, we had a dream to become a Paralympic sport but that seemed a distant possibility at that stage.

At home, Welsh Badminton developed a coach education workshop with Disability Sport Wales, and we slowly started to work more closely with first Scotland, then Ireland and finally the big guns, England and created the 4 Nations. Fiona Reid (now CEO of Disability Sport Wales) and Norman Greenhouse (former WBU Development Officer) were key in creating and delivering the workshops. This started to raise the profile of disability badminton and the development of a series of events proved incredibly successful and offered a positive experience for all areas of disability.

It was at one of these events in Cardiff that I had arranged a meeting with Paul Kurzo (Swiss), who had become President of IBAD (around 2008). We spent 2 whole days discussing and debating about what IBAD could achieve and what we needed to do. We needed help, and we needed help urgently, from the Badminton World Federation (BWF). We knew we needed to gain their support quickly and with the permission of the IBAD committee, along with Günter Klützke (Germany – our Technical guru) we started to develop the partnership with the BWF. In 2009 I (somehow) got voted in as Vice-President of IBAD at the World Championships in Korea. Our work continued with the BWF and in 2010 a MOU (memorandum of understanding) was signed with BWF cementing the partnership.

In 2011 badminton was recognised officially by the International Paralympic Committee (IPC) and the dream appeared a little clearer. IBAD's name had changed to that of the Para-Badminton World Federation (PBWF) focusing on physical disabilities, which drew us even more in line with the BWF. The help and support from BWF were really starting to pay dividends. There was far better communication across their membership and interest in the sport was increasing all the time. Also, in 2011 the PBWF became fully integrated into the BWF and this area of the sport started to receive one very vital element; FUNDING, and proper funding that would make a massive difference to what could be achieved. In 2012 the Sports classes were redefined and reduced after the World Championships in Guatemala and para-badminton was included within BWF's 2012-16 Strategy.

Classification had to become much more professional, and the work involved in creating the new structure was mind blowing. Dr Silvia Albrecht (former Swiss International and Olympian) headed this development and was instrumental in ensuring the sport had a classification system that was appropriate. Silvia and her team of classifiers have done, and continue to do, an amazing service to badminton.

With para-badminton now a key part of the BWF structure, Paul Kurzo became one of the Vice Presidents and I slotted nicely into the newly set up Para-Badminton Commission (or the workers as I like to call them!). This was made up of a host of people from BWF and the para-badminton world and our role was to ensure that the strategy came to life, and we continued to raise the profile across the globe.

Coach Education Workshops were developed and delivered, taking the message and our sport to areas that we felt would make the biggest impact. A small band of coaches took the workshops across the globe and momentum continued. Throughout this phase, the Commission and BWF worked continually on our plan to be included into the Tokyo Paralympics (2020). It's difficult to explain how much work was involved in this process. Key BWF personnel, Stuart Borrie, in particular, as well as the President, Paul-Eric Hoyer Larsen and even a last-minute video from the newly crowned female World Champion, Carolina Marin, ensured that our final presentation to the IPC was a 'nailed on' success. The sport was now destined for its debut in Tokyo in 2020.

The work on the commission intensified and more emphasis was placed on developing the sport across the globe, increasing the playing base, educating coaches and governing bodies as well as creating a tournament structure that could cater for the ever-increasing demand. It was full on.

On the home front, work had continued across the 4 Nations and soon efforts started towards the set-up of a GB programme with the Paralympics in mind. As with all developments, there have been highs and lows both across the 4 Nations and also at the BWF level. That's only natural when you are having to rely on a massive amount of volunteer support to deliver programmes. I have worked with so many great people over the years, each one has played their part in turning our great sport into a Paralympic one. It's always amazing to see so many people across the world doing so much for the love of badminton.

At BWF level, work progresses, and even though Tokyo has been postponed for a year, the development work has never stopped and the continual quest to update and refine the sport, catering to the ever-increasing number of players, is great to be part of. The BWF has delivered where disability is concerned, and I have been incredibly impressed by their commitment to the cause. Paul Kurzo has seen this with me, and we both continue to work on the Commission, with Paul tirelessly leading the way.

In reality, from 1995 to Paralympic inclusion for 2020 is incredibly fast....what a journey!

By Raúl Anguiano

Since birth I have had hemiparesis on the whole right side of my body. I started to play badminton in 1985 through the support and initiative of my family, especially my father Mr. Raúl Anguiano Senior. I enjoyed playing able-bodied badminton for 20 years as it helped me to develop physically, emotionally and socially in many ways. But in 2005 I heard about para-badminton and became interested in competing in it. I am an active player for Guatemala in the SL4 Class.

Competing in para-badminton has been one of the best experiences of my life. From the beginning, I have met so many wonderful people from around the world and got to visit places I never thought I would get to see (four different continents so far!). But at the beginning I was the only athlete to represent the Americas Continent and para-badminton was only active in Asia and Europe. I wanted to help change this to help para-badminton grow in my region and worldwide.

Since 2005 different para-badminton players have asked me, *'When will there be a tournament in Guatemala?'*

At the beginning I really didn't know what to answer, so what I said to them is, *'One day.'*

I knew that para-badminton needed to be active with competitions and players in at least 3 continents to have a chance of becoming a Paralympic Sport but from 2005 to 2009 things stayed the same. I was still the only athlete in this part of the world and para-badminton was still active only in Asia and Europe. All this time players continued to ask me, *when there would be a tournament in Guatemala?*

My answer was the same: *'One day.'*

In the German Para-Badminton International 2009 things started to change because I met a coach from Brazil named Lettison Samorane. He had come to this tournament to see how para-badminton competitions were organised. We talked for a long time, and he told me that in Brazil there was a group of around 20 para-badminton athletes. I was so happy and surprised to hear this! We kept talking, and I told him how important it was for para-badminton to have competitions and players from our region. That's how we made a pact:

*"You, Lettison organise the first Continental Para-Badminton Championships in Brazil in 2010 and I will organise the World Championships in Guatemala in 2011."*

Since that day when people asked me when there will be a tournament in Guatemala my answer is *'World Championships in 2011!'*

I knew there was a lot of work to do, so the first thing I did after returning from Germany was to talk to my dad to ask him if he could help me organise the World Championships in Guatemala. He said 'yes'. The reason I asked my father to help me was because he had been President of the Guatemala Badminton Federation from 1999 to 2007 and was still, at that time, Vice-President of the Pan Am Badminton Confederation. He was a very enthusiastic person and got to work on it immediately. He got the support from the Guatemala Badminton Federation and the Pan Am Badminton Confederation and with that in October of 2009 we went to Korea to compete in the 7th Para-Badminton World Championships (WC).

World Cup host countries are selected via a closed meeting at the location of the previous World Cup. My father and I applied for Guatemala to host the 8th Para-Badminton World Championships in 2011 and we won by a unanimous decision…! Lettison did his part by organising the 1st Pan Am Para-Badminton Championships in Brazil in 2010 with 3 countries Brazil, Peru and Guatemala.

Hosting a tournament like World Championships is really hard work, but through the support and hard work of my family, the Guatemala Badminton Federation, the Badminton Pan Am Confederation and many volunteers from Guatemala we successfully hosted the first and only World Championships celebrated outside of Europe and Asia.

I believe the 8th Para-Badminton World Championships celebrated in my country, Guatemala, were a barrier breaker for our sport for two reasons:

» **It was the first World Championships organised with the full support of the BWF (this changed para-badminton because it gave us the resources for development)**
» **It was the first World Championships outside of Europe or Asia with the participation of more than 20 countries but more importantly athletes from 6 Pan-American countries**

Since then, para-badminton has gone a long way in our region. We have had multiple Para-Badminton internationals (Canada, USA, Peru, Guatemala, Colombia, Brazil and Cuba), there have been five Continental Championships and para-badminton was included for the first time in the Para Pan American Games in Lima. Para-badminton is played in more than 15 countries in our region now and on 7th October 2014 para-badminton was selected as one of the sports of the Tokyo 2020 Paralympic Games and it's a wonderful thing being part of all this.

It was a very difficult task hosting the 2011 WC because there are many stakeholders and things to be taken care of. But in the end, it was worth every second and every effort. I will always remember this as one of the most important things of which I was part, and I am very proud that my family and country are part of it.

## ∽ Don't Shoot, It's Only a Leg! ∽

I am used to wearing my leg continuously for between 15 and 18 hours per day. Once when my father was ill in hospital, I ended up wearing the leg continuously for around 36 hours whilst I stayed by his side. This is manageable because you can always adjust to keep your stump comfortable throughout the day. Not so easy to do on long haul flights like the one to Guatemala which took 23/24 hours and two flights.

The first one was from Heathrow (London) to Miami (USA) and then from there we flew onto Guatemala. It was really tiring. Taking long flights as an above knee amputee is more frustrating than if you are a below knee amputee as you can't just unclip your prosthetic leg as easily. To release the prosthetic (the stump gets really sore the longer you keep the prosthetic on) I'd have to unbutton my trousers which isn't a good thing to do whilst sitting on a plane next to other passengers. They might think I was a secret flasher or slightly unhinged and throw me off the plane, which would have meant missing the chance of a lifetime to compete in Guatemala. A place I'd never been to before. And anyway, even if you do take the prosthetic off the cabin pressure is so high it makes your leg swell so putting it back on is the most painful thing ever, if you can get it on that is, otherwise it's time to sit legless in a wheelchair instead. All in all the leg stayed on for the whole of the 23/24 hour long journey even though it was uncomfortable and the skin became really sore.

We stayed in a big hotel with shopping malls underneath. At the same time we were there, they were holding the 'Miss World' competitions and the competitors were also staying at the hotel. There were plenty of beautiful people dressed very smartly all around us. It was December and they had their Christmas tree up already, so it was a really nice atmosphere. We couldn't go sightseeing anywhere on our own though. It was regarded as a very dangerous place for tourists. To go from the hotel to the badminton hall we were escorted by motorbike convoys and a guide, one each at the back and front of the minibus and one on either side. In a strange way it almost felt like we were as important as a presidential convoy because the guards were with us all the time.

We were strongly advised not to walk around alone outside the hotel. Only thing was that someone forgot to tell one of our team-mates this before he got to Guatemala. He got to the hotel one day ahead of us. There is a beautiful bridge near there and he decided to go there in his wheelchair on his own. In the minibus the day after, he was telling us about the fantastic views from the bridge and our guide just stared at him in disbelief. She gulped and said: *'Do you realise that just 3 days earlier, somebody had their head cut off by bandits on that bridge?'*

Our team-mate's face was an absolute picture! I think we were all kicking ourselves because none of us took a selfie of it. The guide told us that she would be with us wherever we went. Lots of robbery goes on and tourists are easy targets because they obviously look different and stand out from the regular inhabitants. To be fair, wheelchair access was quite good when we were out and about which made up for the rest of it.

The sports hall was in one of the roughest areas you've ever seen. It was very hot inside when the matches were on as there was no air conditioning. They would leave all the fire exit doors open to get air into the hall during matches. To get to the hall there was a very steep incline (at least 75 feet of incline). Wheelchair users had to be pushed up. A few guys tried to wheelchair down, but they would go too quickly and end up banging into a wall. One guy even tried going downhill with his brakes on all the way down. We could see the sparks coming off his wheels and the screeching really jarred our ears. His brakes were a bit wrecked too by the time he got to the bottom of the hill!

The competition hall was in what looked like a very run down, poor shanty town. All around us, wherever we looked, we just got the impression that everyone there was on the edge of poverty. Ladies of 70+ years were so poor they were still working making lace souvenirs. The trucks and buses were all in a poor condition. They would all have failed their MOTs over here I'm sure, but they were very full of people every time we saw them. When you see people living in these conditions you realise how lucky we are in England.

We usually ate at the hotel as that was the safest thing to do whilst we were competing. Gobi Ranganathan, my doubles partner, got a bit of food poisoning which upset his game. Guatemala will always stand out in my memory because it was where I competed as a wheelchair player in an international competition. I was determined and very lucky to have been able to do so, as the classification system was about to undergo a major overhaul in 2012 in order for the sport to be admitted into the Paralympics. Within the old classification system above knee amputees were used to being allowed to play both as standing players and as wheelchair players. The new classification has tightened up the rules and made it clearer for players. In my case, it means that I can compete only as a standing player under the new rules because of the length of my residual stump. That hurt a bit as I was used to competing under the old classification rules which allowed me to compete in a wheelchair and as a standing player but eventually, I came to terms with it. If that is what it would take to get us to the Paralympics, then it was a sacrifice I was prepared to make.

It was a lively annual general meeting (AGM) at that tournament because we knew that we were getting para-badminton closer to the dream. Yet in doing so, we would all be accepting some hard and harsh classification rules which would limit how we could compete in the future.

On the last day of the tournament, we all felt a bit more relaxed and went to look around the zoo with our guide. It was very nice being in a hot country during what is usually a cold and wet December back home. The Guatemalan people are not overly friendly (as compared to the USA) but they are polite and curious about tourists. The wheelchair users sometimes had to be pushed over the cobblestones in the streets, but they didn't mind that. We came across some terraced houses which were striking because they were all one colour in a row. So, there was a row of pink, a row of orange, and so on. It was so strikingly different to how we lived over here that it was worth the extra bit of struggling to experience something that not many disabled tourists would get to see.

The real adventure happened on the way back from the tournament. We landed in Miami airport, tired but happy after our enjoyable tournament. Coming off that flight, I was using the assisted wheelchair airport service and was heading towards the transit lounge which involved going through Customs again. The x-ray machine started beeping as I walked through it because of my metal leg. So, they took me into a room to the side with 3 armed guards; 2 men and 1 woman, to be searched for drugs, weapons or illegal / counterfeit goods that shouldn't be allowed into the country. Intimidating? Scary? You can say that again!

When we got into the room, I was asked to face the guards for some questions. I settled down and tried to make myself comfortable expecting them to take their time with me. Just as they were about to start the questions about which flight I'd just come off, what I'd packed in my luggage etc. my prosthetic knee chose that exact moment to do its party piece. It locked and shot the whole leg upwards, so it looked as though I had an automatic weapon concealed in my trousers! Now I'd experienced this before and sometimes I'd do it just to create a stir whilst with family or friends to get them to laugh. But I didn't expect it to happen without any warning whilst I was being interrogated by armed Customs Officials in Miami coming back from a South American country notorious for its gun violence, drug-smuggling and other criminality.

The guards jumped right out of their skins, looked menacingly straight at me (all 3 of them!) and pointed their guns ready to shoot. I was petrified that they were going to pepper me with bullets all over my whole body, and I'd get flown home in a body bag for my wife to collect from the airport. But a part of me also wondered, if they shot a bullet at the metal part of the leg would it ricochet off and where would it land? What trajectory would it take? Up, down, across, back to the guard and catch him in the arm or heart? And if that one didn't get me the other two guards' bullets sure would, because there would be no time to duck, roll and hide behind anything like they do in the action movies.

So I did the best thing I could think of. I put my hands up quickly and yelled: *'don't shoot, don't shoot, it's a leg, it's only a leg, look!'* Everyone in the room breathed a big sigh of relief. It was all over in less than a minute or two, but it felt like everything was happening in slow motion and I could almost see myself as if I was watching the whole episode from above. The adrenaline was still pumping in my tired brain as they said, *'Don't do that again. It looked to us like a concealed weapon. Because of all the drugs and gun smuggling that goes on in the country you've just travelled from, we tend to shoot first and ask very few questions later.'*

Luckily, they had calmed down sufficiently to let me on the flight back to Heathrow so I didn't have to find a way to explain to Kamalpreet Kaur and my family why I was locked up in a police station in Miami. That would have been another one of those 'conversations you shouldn't have as a married couple.' Yes, there are many tests to a relationship when you have been married as long as we have, but I am glad I didn't have to go through that one. It would have been safer to have been kept locked up in a Miami jail with the key thrown away!

## ∽ We Are In! ∽

It's long been my dream to help get para-badminton into the Paralympics. That is why I stayed and played in one sport for so long. I won't qualify for the para-badminton team that will be competing in Tokyo in 2020 (now 2021 due to the Covid19 pandemic) as I will be too old. My singles rankings are going down now because for the last few years I haven't competed as often in international tournaments. There isn't going to be a men's doubles category of matches in my classification at the Games. If there had been then I may have qualified. It's nice to see all the youngsters coming through, though, and if there is a way in which I can play a part in the Games then I certainly will try to do so.

All the matches that I, and the other disabled badminton players of the 1980's-2014, played around the world contributed to the sport being included in the biggest competition, the Paralympics. It's the one event we all set our hearts on when we started playing all those years ago. We found out in 2014 that the sport had been accepted as a Paralympic sport for Tokyo, Japan 2020. I was in India when I received the short, sweet message on Facebook from Martin Rooke.

*Tokyo Para-Badminton Paralympians:*
*Martin Rooke, Jack Shephard, Krysten Coombs and Daniel Bethell*

'We are in' and I was over the moon. It was an historic, defining moment for all of us who played the game.

Martin Rooke, from our badminton club Herts Toppers, is a serious contender for Tokyo 2020/21. He has made it through the rigorous selection process and has been training for this event for the last 4 years as a singles wheelchair player, WH2 classification. We are keeping our fingers crossed that he makes it through to Tokyo to fly the flag high for Team GB in Para-Badminton. Martin introduced me to wheelchair badminton, and the first time I ever played in a wheelchair against anyone, I ended up in the final with Martin as my opponent.

He obviously outclassed me on that day, but I managed to win the runner's up medal. I enjoyed playing badminton from a wheelchair so much that I entered the English leg of the Four Nations tournament in Stoke Mandeville after that and got my first medal as a wheelchair player. Phoenix Badminton Club sponsored my RGK wheelchair. RGK makes some of the best sports wheelchairs around and it's touching to have their support.

My dream to help get para-badminton into the Paralympics seems to have come true at last. It has been an incredibly emotional time for all of us, especially in 2020 when the full impact of the Covid-19 pandemic became apparent, and the Olympics and Paralympics were put on hold. Everyone in the para-badminton community was devastated. To get so close and then to have it snatched away from us at the last minute. It was deeply unfair. But we didn't give up hope, and for the compact version of the Olympics/Paralympics in Tokyo, September 2021, we are going to do our very best to make sure that para-badminton players have a memorable Games - pandemic or no pandemic. We are IN, and we will WIN!

*Tokyo Para-Badminton Paralympian and Medal Winner: Daniel Bethell.*  *Tokyo Para-Badminton Paralympian and Medal Winner: Krysten Coombs.*

# ∾ A Toilet With a Hot Seat ∾

The Japan Para-Badminton International, 2017 was the nearest to competing in the Paralympics as I'll ever get, I reckon. Going abroad to tournaments always means adventure, fun and excitement. Things just seem to happen to me, and Japan was no different.

I went over there with my son and immediately on landing. We were struck by how totally different it is from anywhere we'd ever been before. Absolutely fascinating. But the first thing we had to do was find our way out of the airport to be met by our hosts. We'd been told to wait by the entrance, so after collecting our luggage off the carousel, we strolled to the big glass doors and looked for people with our name cards. We waited and waited, and I thought that something was up because no one appeared to come and collect us. I finally found someone that spoke some English and Japanese and explained to him that we were here for a para-badminton tournament but seemed to have lost our hosts. He made some enquiries and it turned out that they were waiting at the other entrance for us, so it all worked out in the end.

Getting out of the airport and looking as far as the eye can see, the whole country strikes you as being very clean. There are strict speed limits on the roads with lots of traffic lights. And the toilets even had a hot seat! It certainly made me wonder,

*'Do Japanese people do a lot of work whilst they are on the toilet? Because if we had something like that in my house, none of our family would ever come off it!'*

Another thing I noticed was that they didn't seem to talk to each other whilst out and about. You just see them looking at their notebooks/tablets or mobile phones. Things were well organised over there as far as public transport went. There was a proper queue for the train or bus with people lining up to go in and out as the train stops. In fact, whether they realised it or not, people over there seem to walk in one direction in lines - one way or the other way. All the ticket machines are in Japanese, and the trains were all very punctual. The wheelchair users were impressed with the train system as they were promptly helped into the carriage by staff and met quickly to be helped to get off. It was so efficient and friendly.

The hotel was absolutely amazing. It was very clean, but being a vegetarian in Japan isn't easy. Everyone eats meat or fish so for 2 days I lived off rice and salad until the chef started cooking delicious vegetarian dishes for me.

Our first day was the warmup where we just loosened up all our tight muscles, got some practise games in and generally got to know the courts and the other players. There were only 4 players per group, so we all got a chance to play against each other. In the singles matches I played my first game against the top seeded player, Pramod Bhagat, and my last game against Daisuke Fujihara. They both won (obviously!) but it was inspiring. In the doubles games there was a Spanish boy with cerebral palsy who didn't have a partner to play with, so I played with him. We had some good scoring games. He didn't speak any English but somehow, we understood each other, and it was all really good fun. If this is what the Paralympics version is going to be like in 2020 (2021) then I've had a fantastic taste of it.

# APPENDIX

## Competition Summary

### 1974

Men's doubles evening classes (Able-bodied)

### 1976-1977

Hertfordshire Open Men's Doubles Tournament - Runners Up Stevenage.

Qualified as a badminton coach

### 1978-1979

Flying Feathers Badminton Club (FFBC) Mixed Doubles Tournament - Runners Up –
Orion Hall, Stamford Hill, London

FFBC Men's Doubles Tournament - Semi Final

FFBC Open Men's Doubles Tournament - Champion

## 1974-1980

Won five medals at Middlesex Badminton League, Barnet District Badminton League, Enfield Mixed Badminton League and Hertfordshire Men's Badminton League.

## 1981-1982

Hadley Badminton Club (H.B.C.) Men's Doubles Champion – able-bodied
Only disabled amputee player.

Won men's doubles with partner Harry Thakhar, Barnet

## 1982-1983

H.B.C. Men's Doubles Tournament. Champions. Partner - Mukesh Amin able bodied, Barnet.

H.B.C. Mixed Doubles Tournament - Runners Up

## 1983-1984 able bodied

Barnet District League Mixed Doubles Class 2. Lost in the semi- final. Partner - Joanne Master, FFBC

## 1984-1985 abled bodied

Barnet District League Mixed Doubles Class 2. Lost in the semi- final. Partner - Joanne Master. Orion Hall, Stamford Hill, London

## 1985 – Para-Badminton Stoke Mandeville, Aylesbury

BASA National Games - Gold medal Weightlifting, Gold medal
400 metres running

National running record of 3 minutes.15.3 seconds for 400 metres. Stoke Mandeville, Aylesbury

Badminton Men's Singles - opponent Richard Court, Gloucester -
lost best of 3 games against him.

## 1985-1986 – Able bodied. Orion Hall Stamford Hill, London

F.F.B.C. Men's Doubles Tournament. Semi-final

Participated in Barnet Badminton League Annual Men's Doubles Handicap Tournament.

### 1986 – Para -Badminton: British Amputee Sports Association. Stoke Mandeville, Aylesbury

B.A.S.A. National Games. Badminton - Men's Doubles Tournament - Gold medal. Partner Michael Dooner.

400 metres running - Gold medal - new national record 2 minutes 40.7 seconds

### 1987-1988 – Para-Badminton Stoke Mandeville, Aylesbury

B.A.S.A. National Games. Badminton Men's Doubles Gold, Badminton Men's Singles Silver. Weight Lifting Silver.

### 1989 – Para-Badminton Stoke Mandeville, Aylesbury

B.A.S.A. National Games. Badminton Men's Singles - runner up

Men's Doubles - disqualified

### 1990 – Para-Badminton Stoke Mandeville, Aylesbury

B.A.S.A. National Games. Badminton Men's Singles - Gold

Men's Doubles Finals - Runner up

400 metres running - Silver

100 metres running - Runner up.

### 1991- Para -Badminton, Stoke Mandeville, Aylesbury

National Amputee Games - Badminton Men's Doubles - winner Partner Frances Morrison.

Men's Singles - Runner up

### 1994 – Laying the foundations to the Paralympics

Dutch Tournament

Mixed Doubles - runner up - (2 close games 15-12 and 15-13)

Men's singles - reached Semi finals

British Open Swindon - reached semi- finals in singles and doubles

## 1995

National Federation Amputee Games, Stoke Mandeville, Aylesbury.
Mixed Doubles - Gold

Men's Singles - reached semi finals

Running - 400metres - Gold - time 3 minutes 5seconds.
100m and 200m - Silver medals in both.

European Games - Stoke Mandeville – IBAD formed in 1995. First time Dr Jim Mackay
(Wales) invited other countries to England.

Mixed Doubles - Gold
Men's Singles - Silver
Men's Doubles - Silver

Enfield Men's League – Men's doubles - Runners up. – Able bodied. Annual tournament –
Enfield Drill Hall, Old Army Barracks.

## May 1996 – Para-Badminton

National Federation Games

> British Open -- Men's Singles – Gold - Swindon.

> Mixed Doubles - Silver

## 1997 Para-Badminton

October - European Championships Dortmund, Germany.

Men's Doubles (above waist handicap) - Gold

Men's Singles (below waist handicap) - 3rd

Enfield Badminton League Tournament – able bodied
Men's Doubles - 4th

## 1998 – Able bodied – Hadley Badminton Club, High Barnet

H.B.C. Men's Doubles - Runners up
Mixed Doubles - lost in semi finals

Enfield Badminton League Tournament (against able bodied players)
Group Tournament – Men's Doubles. Runners up – able bodied.

November - Amersfoort, The Netherlands - Para-Badminton World Championships.

Below Waist Men's Singles - 4<sup>th</sup>

Doubles - won 3 games out of 5 but did not qualify to go further.

## 1999 Para-Badminton

November - European Championships, Tel Aviv, Israel.
Men's Doubles - Bronze.

## 2000 – Para-Badminton World Championships, Borken, Germany

Men's singles and Men's doubles - no medals

## 2003

August - World Para-Badminton championships Cardiff, Wales.
Men's Doubles - Gold - Partner Colin Broadbridge

September - European Para badminton Championship Bitburg, Germany.

Men's singles and Men's doubles AK standing category.

## 2004

European Para-Badminton Championship, Tilburg, Netherlands.

## 2006

May - European Para-Badminton Open, Dortmund, Germany

August - Four Nations Para-Badminton Championships, Cardiff, Wales

Men's Singles – Silver
Men's Doubles - Gold - Partner Anthony Forster.

September - European Para-Badminton Championships, Seville, Spain.

Men's Doubles - Bronze - Partner William Smith

## 2007

May – European Para-Badminton Open Dortmund, Germany

Men's Singles - competed with no medal

Men's Doubles - Bronze

August - World Para-Badminton Championship, Bangkok, Thailand

August - Four Nations' Para-Badminton Championships, Cardiff, Wales.

Men's Doubles - Gold - Partner - Anthony Forster

Middlesex Integrated Tournament (Abled and Disabled)

Men's Doubles - Gold

Men's Singles - Bronze

## 2008 Para-badminton

February - Four Nations' Para-badminton Championships, Largs, Scotland

Men's Doubles – Gold - Partner Bruno Forbes

May - European Para-badminton Championships Open, Dortmund, Germany.

Men's Doubles - Bronze

November Four Nations Para-Badminton Championship, Dublin, Ireland.

Men's Doubles –– Silver - Partner Daniel Lee

## 2009 First time Badminton England hosted the Four Nations Para-Badminton Championships

May - Four Nations Para-Badminton Championships, Liverpool

Men's Doubles - Gold. Partner Bruno Forbes. Men's Singles - no medal

September - joined BSCA Badminton Club, Queen Elizabeth Girl's School, Barnet.

This is an able bodied club. I am the only disabled person in the whole club.

## 2010

May - European Para-Badminton Championships, Filzbach, Switzerland

August - UKSA (Sikh Association) Able Bodied Tournament, Chigwell.

Men's Doubles - Gold.

## 2011

January - Middlesex Disability Tournament, Heston.

Men's Doubles - Gold. Partner Daniel Lee

May – English leg of the Four Nations' Para-Badminton Championships (Wheelchair) Aylesbury England.

Men's Singles – Silver – playing in a wheelchair. Lost to Martin Rooke in the final. Only had 6 weeks training. First time competing and winning a medal in a wheelchair.

June – UKSA (United Khalsar Sport Academy) Sporting Achievement Award, Chigwell
August - Devon Wheelchair Open.

Men's Singles - reached quarter finals.

November - World Championships Guatemala City, Guatemala (wheelchair category only.)
Men's Singles and Men's Doubles - Partner Gobi Ranganathan

Four Nations' Para-Badminton Championships, Belfast, Northern Ireland. Standing. 1st time 4 amputees on court in the finals.

Men's Doubles - Silver - Partner - Bobby Griffin

## 2012

May - Four Nations' Para-Badminton Championships, Nottingham, England

Wheelchair doubles, Robin Hood Championships - Silver

Partner Martin Rooke

June - European Championship Open, Dortmund, Germany

Men's Doubles - Bronze - Partner Niall Jarvie (Scotland)

British Sikh Council UK, Wolverhampton - Sporting Achievement Award

## 2013

January - Herts County Wheelchair Championship, Hatfield, Herts Sports Village

Mixed Doubles - Bronze

April - Spanish International Para-Badminton Tournament, Villajoyosa, Spain.

SL3 Men's singles and Men's doubles

May - Four Nations' English Para-Badminton Championships, (English leg) Chigwell, Essex.

Men's Singles - Half Court – Silver – standing.

World Para badminton Championships, Dortmund Men's Singles and Men's Doubles.

## 2015 Para-badminton

March - Spanish International, Alcudia, Majorca, Spain – Bronze.

Partner Frank Dietel (Germany) - Men's mixed classification doubles, total category points had to equal 8. I was SLD3 and my partner was SU5 which is the most severe category you can be in (N.B. The "3" of SL3 plus the "5" of SU5 gave the necessary total of 8).

July – Promoting Disability in the Punjab. Disabled mud wrestling. Beat my opponent. Featured on Indian TV and the local newspaper.

September - Para-Badminton BWF World Championship Stoke Mandeville, Aylesbury Men's singles and Men's doubles standing SL3

Limb Power Games 10th year celebration event – badminton workshops. 8th year as volunteer coach. Stoke Mandeville, Aylesbury.

Limb Power Mini Marathon Fundraiser - £2300 raised to help young amputees into sport (inc. Gift Aid) Stoke Mandeville, Aylesbury.

## 2016

Nominated as Sports Mentor of the Year by the British Sikh Council UK, Coventry as a special thanks for contribution to sports

10th European Para-badminton Championship - Beek-Limburg, The Netherlands - competed.

August – Limb Power Mini Marathon. Stoke Mandeville, Aylesbury. Raised £1076 to help young amputees into sport

## 2017

Japan International Para-Badminton Championships, Tokyo SL3 Men's singles and Men's doubles (standing)

Limb Power Fundraiser– Climbed O2 Arena

## 2019

April Limb Power 10K Brighton Marathon Fundraiser

June 'Walk for the Ward', Royal Free and Barnet Hospitals Trust 5K Fundraiser

July Sheffield,. Inaugural UK Para-Badminton Championships.

## 2020

February Limb Power Fundraiser – Climbed O2 Arena

February Cancer Research UK 10K Marathon – official event cancelled due to weather but we did the distance individually on 8th Feb.

February Worcester Weekend Sportsday. Two different partners, both novices. To promote disability/inclusive sport.

Spanish Para-Badminton International, Cartagena, Spain - March 8th-15th – cancelled due to Covid 19.


## 2014-2019

Nanak Darbar Gurudwara (Sikh Temple) North London Badminton Tournament. I organise this every 2 years and run the classes. Once per week every Wednesday.


## Badminton Clubs Founded

1983-1984 season Harry Thakhar, Charlie Chogley and I formed the Mill Hill Badminton Club. The club lasted 6 seasons. Able bodied club. I was the only disabled player.

2005-2007 Burnt Oak Leisure Centre – there was already a badminton club there. We tried to integrate disabled and able bodied players into one club.

2012 and continuing. Herts Toppers Badminton Club formed with Martin Rooke and Gobi Ranganathan.

(*https://en-gb.facebook.com/HertsToppers/*) Herts Toppers Men's 4 (South West Region) League Results:

> 2012-13 5th in league (first season competing as a club) 2013-14 4th
>
> 2014-15 2nd
>
> 2015-16 1st

Unbeaten 9 wins, 1 draw. 140 games played. 100 won, 40 lost

> 2016-17 2nd
>
> 2017-18 3rd

By default. Penalty due to a player not filling his name on the entrance form correctly.

> 2018-19 1st
>
> 2019-2020 We are currently 2nd in the league. Suspended as a consequence of Covid19.

Since 2005 I have been playing for the Middlesex Masters able bodied club, the first Saturday of every month. Invitation only club. I am the only amputee player.

## Badminton Organisations

Badminton World Federation: *https://bwfbadminton.com/*

Badminton England: *https://www.badmintonengland.co.uk/*

Badminton Scotland: *http://www.badmintonscotland.org.uk/*

Badminton Wales: *https://www.badminton.wales/*

Ulster Branch Badminton Union of Ireland: *https://www.ulsterbadminton.com*

Badminton Europe: *http://www.badmintoneurope.com/Cms/*

## Suppliers of Badminton Equipment (Non-Exclusive List)

RGK: *https://rgkwheelchairs.com/*

Carlton: *https://ukstore.carltonsports.com/*

Yonex: *http://www.yonex.co.uk/*

Ashaway: *https://goode-sport.co.uk*

## Amputee and Sikh Charities and Disability Aids Providers (Non-Exclusive List)

Douglas Bader Foundation: *https://www.douglasbaderfoundation.com*

LimbPower: *https://limbpower.com*

Arctic One: *https://arctic1.co.uk*

WheelPower: *https://www.wheelpower.org.uk/*

Blatchford: *https://www.blatchford.co.uk*

Pace Rehabilitation: *https://pacerehab.com*

Sikh Role Model: *https://sikhrolemodel.com*

## Book Sponsors

Major Builders: majorbuilders@aol.com

Dr Zak's Pumping Iron Gym: www.pumpingironfitnessgym.com

Humming Bird Kia: https://www.kia.com/uk/dealers/hummingbirdkia/

Blatchford: https://www.blatchford.co.uk

# About the Author

**Meva Singh Dhesi** (aged 67 years at the time of writing) lives in Totteridge, North London with his wife. He has 5 children, 4 girls, 1 boy, and 2 grandchildren. He came to the UK at the age of 13 with his mother, brother and two sisters. A car accident on 2nd July 1980, when he was 25 years old, resulted in him becoming an amputee. Thanks to Waheguru ji (God) for giving him the willpower and motivation to overcome the limitations of his disability. He has not let anything get in the way of his love of badminton or his family from those early beginnings right through to the present day. Despite his acquired disability he continues to be an active member of his able- bodied badminton club Barnet South Community Association (BSCA); playing there every Friday evening as well as playing with Herts Toppers. He is the only Sikh amputee in the UK to have competed in para-badminton tournaments at local, national and international level as a standing player and as a wheelchair player at an international tournament.

Connect with Meva via his website and dream of being in Team GB.
Meva Singh Dhesi, Para-Badminton:

*http://mevasinghdhesi.uk*
Website courtesy of Benjamin James Singh Ward.

Be inspired to succeed!